A SYMPHONY OF LOGIC FROM THE "BASKET OF DEPLORABLES"

SECULARISM, RACISM, MONEY

CORNELIUS VAN BLYDERVEEN

WESTBOW
PRESS®
A DIVISION OF THOMAS NELSON
& ZONDERVAN

This book is a work of non-fiction. Unless otherwise noted, the author
and the publisher make no explicit guarantees as to the accuracy of
the information contained in this book and in some cases, names of
people and places have been altered to protect their privacy.

WestBow Press books may be ordered through booksellers or by contacting:

WestBow Press
A Division of Thomas Nelson & Zondervan
1663 Liberty Drive
Bloomington, IN 47403
www.westbowpress.com
844-714-3454

All Scripture quotations are taken from the King James Version.

ISBN: 978-1-6642-2870-2 (sc)
ISBN: 978-1-6642-2871-9 (e)

Print information available on the last page.

WestBow Press rev. date: 01/10/2022

PREFACE

Know Yourself

This book is for everyone in the world. It should be translated into every language. This book is for the presidents, prime ministers, senators, members of Congress, and members of parliament. This book is for kings and queens. It is also for those who live on skid row, the homeless on the street, and everyone in between.

This book is a defence of the Covenant, the Covenant of grace, as opposed to its imitation, the Social Contract. This book is not religious, nor is it about religion. It is about the inescapability of religion. If you think you may be a victim, you are probably right, and this book is for you. If you think you might be a predator, you are also probably right, and this book is for you. Knowledge is transforming and liberating; ideology hates knowledge and liberty. Buy this book before it is banned. If and when ideology gets its way, academic freedom will be totally banned. Any attempt to ban this book is anti-Semitism and anti-intellectual. To ban research into anti-Semitism is anti-Semitism.

This book is by no means everything that could be said and written on this subject. You may take it, apply it, and expand it. It is intended that this book be the starting point for critique of contemporary western society in the twenty first century. It is intended for dialogue not repression.

Forgive my errors and omissions if the there are any in this book.

I tried my best; errors can be corrected, and omissions can be added. Join us by putting knowledge to work. Enter our discussions and engage the world, making it a better place.

Thanks to all of those who work in the information industry and the news media who can yet be objective about reality and report facts as they are. We need more like you.

Thanks to all of those who write books, being sincere about truth and allowing discernment about what is objective and what is not.

Thanks to my dear wife for her patience, once she discovered I was writing a book she understood why I was not always there and didn't hear.

Thanks be to God for the quiet time and grace to read, think, and write.

1

WHY A SYMPHONY OF LOGIC?

Music in the present moment can never be heard; it is only a single sound. Hearing music requires a memory of the sound in the past moment, creating anticipation for the next moment, and then being confirmed in the present moment. Only then do you hear music. Like they say, "It's just in the mind." The present hardly exists. The present is the point of transition in the midst of eternity where the future becomes the past. If you have no memory of the past, you would be paralyzed and could have no expectations for the future. Logic, like music, cannot exist without context. It can only act upon the knowledge of the past; when there is no knowledge of the past, there is no logic. If you do not know our history, then there can be no logical expectation for the future. Yes, you need to learn your history. You will have a much better life and only then will you begin to hear the music.

Have you ever asked, what are we missing? With all that we have and are doing in life, in society, and in government, all at the present, what are we missing and overlooking that should be obvious and beneficial, but we are not achieving? Are we missing out on the best?

When Christopher Columbus discovered the West Indies in 1492, and Cortez later arrived in the western hemisphere, they found a continent populated with millions of people who had developed a civilization much different from that of Europe and the Middle East. Here was a civilisation that had not invented the wheel. No one thought of putting two wheels on an axle for transportation, hence humans carried almost everything. Gold was used to worship the gods, and cocoa beans were used as money. There was no alphabet to write with, only picture symbols. However, they did invent something very remarkable and for this they used the wheel—an accurate calendar that consisted of three wheels that turned towards one another. The wheels were marked with pointers to indicate time. It was a system of keeping track of all the events in the solar system. This calendar allowed the elite, the priests, to accurately predict the seasons, the beginning of the rainy season and dry season, the winter and summer solstices, as well as the eclipses of the sun and moon.

Now the priests could teach the people that the seasons depended on their behaviour and human sacrifices to the gods. The priests required human sacrifices for everything; nothing happened or could be done without sacrifice. For the rainy season they required human sacrifices so the rain would come. They required human sacrifices to bring the eclipses and show the people that the priests had a token from the gods. However, the rainbow was considered an evil omen; it was not predictable, so it was not useable by the priests; apparently they had no pride.

When the rainy season did not come, it meant the gods were angry, and more human sacrifices were needed. They offered the gods only a human heart cut out of the chest of a live human. The heart was laid atop of a stone altar to bake in the sun. All this was done on top of the pyramid temples. The remaining bodies were cast on heaps of rotting and stinking corpses. Eventually the whole city began to stink. Finally the rain came, and the sacrifices stopped. It was a religion in which cruelty was the ultimate in religious piety.

They had the most successful climate religion the world has ever seen. However, then the Spanish came. Incensed with indignation at the cruelty of the human sacrifices, they threw down the idols from the pyramid temples, banished the human sacrifices, and stole the gold. Climate religion came to an end. The seasons came and went, the eclipses came at their determined times, and the civilization disappeared.

Were the Mayans missing out on something, or are we missing

out on something? What kind of people do we want to be? What future do we want together?

Much of this symphony I am writing is from my own life experience. It began in Jerusalem on a Sunday morning in February 2005 at the Western Wall, or *Ha Kotel*, as in Hebrew. I was there to pray. I prayed for the peace of Jerusalem, for Zion, for Israel, for the Covenant, and for the condition of the world. I prayed for forgiveness and salvation, knowledge and wisdom. I prayed that the prayers of everyone who prayed for these things in Jerusalem would also have their prayers answered. I am confident that I am not alone in this. There are millions like me who come there to pray because they know the self-evident value, love, and salvation that is in the Covenant. I dedicated myself to the Lord for His purpose in whatever way that might be.

The conclusion of this prayer at Jerusalem was to educate myself on the issues and then wait patiently but actively on the Lord. In this regard, I made it my mission to find the cause and origin of anti-Semitism, to find if there was a predictable pattern established throughout history.

Anti-Semitism is a phenomenon of hatred of the Jew that is more than three thousand years old and is worldwide; it follows the Jews wherever they are. It is a phenomenon that has been as constant over time as if it were the weather and the climate. Why? This I now needed to know and will find out as best I can.

This led me to reading more books, but now doing so with a purpose. I read history, economics, philosophy, and apologetics. Above all, I read the Bible, both as history and as the Word of God. By now I could write my own philosophy book, but it would take years to write. I also need to earn a living, and when my book is finished, I'm sure no one will read it. So instead I'll write this short book, a symphony of logic from the basket of deplorables. I think everyone with some knowledge of history will understand it.

Now why from the, "basket of deplorables"? In case we forgot, it was Hillary Clinton who, during a fundraising speech in her

2016 US presidential campaign, called half of Donald Trump's supporters, "a basket of deplorables." When we recognize her ideological tyranny, contempt, and bigotry, as well as that coming from the liberal ideological elite and academia she represents, then such a designation is a badge of honor. They have just proven that their intolerant ideological tyranny and its intent are true. She gave us a token of vindication.

This reminds me of the confederacy of Calvinist Dutch nobles in 1566. They came to the Court of the Governess, Margaret of Parma, who represented the Habsburg King Philip II of Spain. There they were called *Les Gueux*, which means beggars. The French Les Gueux became the Dutch *Geuzen* because they asked her to stop the inquisition and persecution of the Protestants. They were people of no value to them, (the ideological elite of the day), so why should these beggars have tolerance? The name "Beggars" stuck, and it was used as their resistance identity, which eventually defeated King Philip II in war and established the Dutch Republic.

Now concerning anti-Semitism, I will tell you here at the beginning of this book what I have found after all those years. Anti-Semitism is a profound hatred of the Covenant—the Supremacy of God and the Rule of Law: (I am your God, you are my people), the Covenant theme repeated throughout the Bible—and an inordinate love for ideology, which is the same as the ancient idolatry. It serves the same purpose, defined as the supremacy of man (humankind) and the rule of tyranny. What you need to know to understand anti-Semitism correctly (logically) is that if there was not a Covenant, there would be no Jew. The Jew becomes the object of the Covenant, an organic association with the Covenant that has no regard for what the Jew may believe about himself or herself or the Covenant. This cuts right through the Gentiles and Jews as well. There is no difference between Jew and Gentile. Yes, we need a major repentance and a return to the Covenant.

Now for the rest of this book I will, from my life experience, show you what the Covenant is and what it is not, and how it relates to what I have learned from history and the Bible.

4

2

DISCOVERING THE COVENANT

In 1979 I married the girl I loved. I could not imagine myself living alone. I needed a wife with whom to share my life, believing that together we are stronger. Marriage is a covenant relationship with each other in the context of a larger covenant of reality and community. Love, like faith, is dead without works. The Covenant is faith, love, and work that are reciprocal. And when we fail, we restore. The Covenant's ultimate achievement is the glory of God by His creation.

We were a young happy couple and excited to get married. We had many things we needed to get ready. We needed a house. Buying a house requires an income and financing; we needed a mortgage. My spouse-to-be worked in health care, and I worked on the family farm. We had apple orchards, strawberry fields, and a tree nursery. The plan was that my fiancée and I would buy a farm, which then would be added to our family farming business. It was 150 acres with a large brick house that had been built in 1870; it was full of beautiful chestnut wood trim. We were excited about our new home. This was 1979. It should have been the best of times, but it was made to be the worst of times. As the year proceeded, the interest rate on mortgages was going up at about 1 per cent per week. It peaked at 21 per cent for a first mortgage. We could not afford our purchase and did not close the deal. Instead we bought a mobile home, which was placed on one of our family farms, and there we lived for the next seven years.

What was wrong in 1979? Our friend's mortgage came up for renewal. After having paid it for five years, they abandoned their house as they could not afford the 21 per cent interest on the renewed mortgage. Many farms and businesses were going bankrupt. All the grain elevators in the country were bankrupt. Who can afford 21 per cent interest on storing grain? It was the time of the penny auctions; banks were foreclosing on farms and trying to sell off the assets and equipment at public auction. Rather naïve in an environment where all the farmers are faced with the same adverse monetary policy. Farmers and farm-related businesses agreed to work together and not bid more than a penny at a time at these auctions. Of course the auctions failed. The banks retreated, and the auctions were discontinued. Then the provincial and federal governments established the Farm Debt Review Board to mitigate farm debt. Rural Ontario did not recover for another ten years, and many of us never recovered. When you go bankrupt, you also get a bad credit rating, which is like a debtor's prison. You are forbidden to recover and punished for a failed monetary system.

The real failure was not with the economy but with monetary policy, a self-important and incompetent monetary elite trying to preserve the value of global monetary capital that exists at the expense of expanding the economy. It was a time of post-war immigration and the post-war baby boom, all needing jobs and houses. No monetary provision had been made for it; the expert elites were too concerned that the world would run out of oil, and climate alarmists were predicting an ice age.

By 1960, every municipality across the country was scrambling to find the money and resources to build new schools. With all the post-war babies, the one-room schoolhouse became obsolete. It was too small; we needed new schools with at least one classroom for each grade. You would think knowing this would give you foresight to do some economic and monetary planning because these children would be growing up and need money, jobs, and houses in the near future. I am sure there were lots of lefties in the 1960 because communism's popularity was growing with a minority at that time. They were screaming, "I told you! You should make abortion legal; the world is getting overpopulated."

Growing up, I was well aware of the negative impact of government on the family and small business through monetary policy, fiscal policy, and social policy. I soon developed a low opinion for government in general and ideological academia in particular. There certainly is no recognizable covenant relationship here.

To comment on the 1970's; we did not have inflation, not in the sense of monetary attrition. We had price increases caused by supply shortages which can be traced to a shortage of investment money. Then there was the oil shock or oil crisis, a major price increase for oil, which in turn increased the cost price of everything. To fight these price increases as if it is inflation with restrictive monetary policy employing high interest rates and price controls was exactly the wrong thing to do. To accommodate higher prices and shortages you need to find more money - to pay the bills and capital for investment to increase supply production. There are two things that could have been done, borrow back the oil money or expand the money supply. Both of these should have been done simultaneously. Instead we were made to suffer. The 1970's became a crisis because of the past failure to expand the money supply in the 1960's to encourage investment.

In 1969, as a young boy, I remember the raging debate about legalizing abortion. It was my introduction to politics. I joined Right to Life. We objected to legalizing abortion under vague criteria such as reasons of health. We knew that this would be the slippery slope to abortion on demand. They assured us it would never happen as there were many safeguards in place for consent to prevent this from happening. Now what do we have today? No abortion law at all; abortion is legal up until birth for any or no reason at all. It has become legalized infanticide.

The Canadian government has blood on its hands for the infanticide and femicide (legal sex-selection abortion). The ideology that has always claimed to defend women's rights has now become the defender of the ultimate in woman hate. There is no covenant here but rather a social contract to kill the unwanted.

So now what does this ideology do with these unwanted people who are pro-life? Do we add them to this contract? I remember all too well from the 1970s and '80s the hate coming from the Toronto pro-choice demonstrators in support of the abortionist Henry Morgentaler, by whose efforts the abortion laws were struck down in our courts. The pro-choice, being counter-demonstrators against the pro-life group, their message was clear. Their signs and language were laced with profanity telling us to, "Abort God from your mind." They know very well that abortion is murder, and their ultimate target is truth, God, and the rule of law.

The social contract is the ideological imitation of the biblical Covenant. Since it is founded on the supremacy of man (or in modern racist terms "humankind") and not God, It feels it is exempt from reality—from creation—and therefore, reserves the right to be arbitrary, contradictory, and self-refuting. All of this will serve as justice and becomes the replacement for the rule of law. In time it all adds up to confusion and self-doubt. In contrast, what is so significant about the biblical Covenant, the Supremacy of God, is that it requires us to be objective concerning creation, reality, justice, and the rule of law. Only then can justice be non-contradictory, non-self-refuting, and the arbitrariness becomes irrelevant, merging into a person's self-governance on logic. It is the foundation of our civil confidence.

If you think we are a secular state, how is ideology secular? How is paganism secular? In order to have a secular state we need the supremacy of God and the rule of law, the requirement to be objective concerning the reality of creation and justice. We need the Covenant. Without this you have a pagan tyranny or a transitional dysfunctional state returning to pagan state religion. Secularism is not secular, it again is a religion; and at this point I may as well also add Judaism is not Jewish. The traditions of people and commentary upon commentary on the Torah and the scriptures are not the covenant. Christians have the same problem; much of it can be ideology and not the covenant.

The philosopher John Locke had it right when he stated that natural rights are inalienable, and therefore, the rule of God supersedes government authority (the rule of man). What John Locke means is the objective reality of God's creation supersedes the vain imagination of man and his tyranny. Any government legislating ideological fantasy into law—setting humanity, nature, and reality on its head—requiring a mandatory spiritual faith in order to make it effectual, abrogates all its authority, and is superseded by the rule of God.

The US Constitution also has it right. The framers of the Constitution knew what they were doing, had read John Locke, and had a good understanding of the Bible. Notwithstanding hereditary racist slavery being an evolving new ideological invention of their contemporary time; this was a problem postponed to the future. It required Abraham Lincoln and the Civil War to defeat slavery—also all within the same context of reality, the Covenant and the supremacy of God—as opposed to racist ideology of a social contract from the supremacy of man.

At one time we all used to think the Ten Commandments from the Bible were relevant in the public forum. However, today they appear to be all but banned from the public by ideologues and their political correctness. How are these Ten Commandments religious and not also secular or civil? What you need to do is write the opposite and enforce that as the rule of law. Then see what you get. To a large degree that is what ideology is doing and is also the reason they do not want to see them. They reveal their sins. The Ten Commandments destroy their alternate reality. The outcome of keeping the Ten Commandments is mercy, then without them we can expect a merciless existence.

3

WHAT IS A BIBLICAL WORLD VIEW?

If we are to live under a biblical Covenant, we need to know what a biblical world view is, and how it can be active and effective in the world.

Should we not, in this world give credit where credit is due and rebuke where rebuke is due without respect of person?

When Donald Trump won the US presidential election in 2016, there was so much hysteria about it caused by the shock among the ideological left that he actually won. I thought I would do some of my own research on him and the people who hate him as well.

I searched the internet for the church affiliation of Donald Trump. I knew from reading his book "Crippled America, How to make America great again", that he grew up as a Presbyterian in New York. However, I wanted to see if there was more I could find out. In my search, several articles from the *Guardian* also came up.

One of them, published Sunday, February 18, 2019, was titled, "Under Trump the American Religious Right is Rewriting its Code of Ethics." "From scorning immigrants to accepting the president's profanity, evangelicals are proving just how flexible their values can be," wrote Randy Balmer, professor in religion at Dartmouth College. It is a rebuke of Christians, and how could they ever vote for Trump? They compromise everything it is to be Christian. Then he listed everything Donald Trump is, beginning with, "He is a liar."

Lying is all right as long as it serves a higher purpose.

It's no problem being married more than well, twice.

Immigrants are scum.

Vulgarity is a sign of strength and resolve.

White lives matter (much more than others).

There is no harm in spending time with porn stars.

It's all right for adults to date children.

The ends justify the means.

All these titles were embellished with mockery for Christians and Donald Trump, all off the wall and that I do not want to repeat.

The first thing I noticed was that Balmer thinks Christianity follows a self-defined and self-imposed code of ethics. Then where is the Bible? The Bible is central to evangelical Christians. But Balmer doesn't want to know this, and he hopes the readers will not notice either because it doesn't fit his narrative. He wants us to be narrow-minded ideologues that follow a code because then we are defeatable. However, when we put the Bible first, we may get stuck with something like that we find in Psalm 119 AKJV: "I have seen an end of all perfection, but thy commandment is exceeding broad."

When we as Christians participate in a democracy, we have limited choices. We do not have the mandate of the government. The choices that we make are not with respect of any person but with respect to God's will for humanity. Therefore, we give credit where credit is due and rebuke where rebuke is due, without respect of person. All this matters and it determines our choices.

When Donald Trump promises to defend the Constitution by appointing judges who will uphold the Constitution and objective human rights in the face of the encroaching ideology, we give him credit for this and our support. What does the alternate choice have to offer? More ideological judges, changing justice and the US Constitution into the tyranny of ideology? This alone, apart from how sincere Trump may be in this promise—that it's not some political hoax—is sufficient to support him, these being the only two choices. We can pray for him, also for Congress and Senate as well our nation and country. We can also engage all of them in government after the election on the same principles.

This I understand to be the active Christian or biblical world view that God will use for His purpose, working one step at a time with as many resources as possible and a lot of patience. Always being a witness for truth and it's reality in any situation. We are not deranged hopeless people, we recognize repentance, forgiveness, and restoration.

Apparently for this writer and the *Guardian* as well, none of this is considered; it must be all nonsense. They do not see any threat to our justice, and what they see in Hillary Clinton they don't say. What they really are saying to Christians is this: Your moral values are too good for the public process, so don't participate in it. And if you do, you are a hypocrite who compromises your values; better keep your religion private. Keep truth in unrighteousness.

At the end of the article, they beg for money because they are an independent news organization that is influenced by no one, no special interests. Then they state they are progressive. They write, "*Guardian* journalism is rooted in facts with a progressive perspective on the world." Progressive *Guardian* and a progressive professor in religion?

So what do these progressives have as a progressive world view? They don't have one. They only have a God-view. The world with all its evil is god, and God is the servant. They will tell God what to do and us how to serve them. We need to be subjugated. That's their view. And yes, they are progressive, first the world is god, then the world with all its evil is god, then the evil world is god, and finally evil is god. In reality these elitist progressive ideologists are the ultra-pious religious fanatics of our time, trying to establish a pagan state religion through the courts and government. The notion of being objective appears to be completely lost.

Another very good reason for supporting Donald Trump that the writer doesn't mention: Should Christians or anyone of any moral integrity support free trade over fair trade? There is nothing fair with a hybrid communist-capitalist totalitarian state such as China. Do we have free trade with a criminal enterprise? Should capitalism now contract a communist labour force to replace our labour force for their capitalist profit? Do we surrender to totalitarianism? Apparently the progressives would.

One more concern on the same subject. I am beginning to hear those who hate us use against us arguments that sound a lot like the weaponization of the grace and mercy from the New Testament Sermon on the Mount. We are to give place and yield to the abuse of those who hate us as the new normal and the New Testament justice—the double standard, one for the Christian and Jew, and another for themselves, the progressive Christian. We are to back down from defending truth and justice, like this quote taken from the Sermon on the Mount, "But I say unto you that you resist not evil." We are neither to be the salt of the world nor the light of the world. We are to shut down. God is love so, therefore, approves of all evil. How could you be so unloving as to hate sin? You would hurt someone's feelings. And then should not Christians and Jews suffer for their faith? Sorry, but this is not what the Sermon on the Mount is about.

Rather, the Sermon on the Mount is a defence of righteousness, the moral law, and objective justice. Our lives and feelings should be confirmation of all this, as illustrated in the following quote from the Sermon on the Mount: "Judge not, that ye be not judged, for with what judgment ye judge ye shall be judged; and with what measure ye mete it shall be measured to you again" (Matthew 7:1, 2, AKJV). Justice is an objective equality. What you think to do to another, you give them the right to do to you. And when they don't, it's a mercy. Mercy is never anyone's right; nor is it a replacement for justice. When we understand the Bible and logic (which is also very much biblical), we will defend objective truth and justice according to their real equality in creation. In the defence of justice, we include ourselves knowing we are to obey God rather than Man—objective truth in creation rather than human fantasy—and knowing vengeance belongs to God and is reserved until a time their iniquity is full. Then we will have justice and retribution. Justice is ongoing but can also be reserved. Yes, at some point justice will be delivered.

Human life exists in cause, effect, and consequences and consequences again give rise to cause. There is a need to be objective. Progress is only made when we redeem the cause, (not just once but every hour). Without redeeming the cause life is a cyclical tragedy.

If there were no Old Testament, there could not be a New Testament. And without the Ten Commandments, there could not be the Sermon on the Mount. What is there of the Ten Commandments that we should not keep today, or what is there of them that we should reverse? Jesus Christ is a Saviour who came to fulfill the law for righteousness, not to abolish the law for grace and life. The moral law is as much grace as the Sermon on the Mount. The Sermon on the Mount is the evidence of the application of the moral law in life. It is about the righteousness of the moral law. Yes, we will suffer for righteousness, for righteousness is an offence to the love of sin, and Jesus Christ is our righteousness. The outcome of the Moral Law is God's mercy.

Those who weaponize scripture and take it out of context are trying to revive the same Nazification theology of the German Christian movement of 1930–1945. It was a theological construction that de-emphasised human sinfulness in order to be, in their opinion, a positive Christianity. Then they also removed all Jewish elements from the New Testament and excluded the Old Testament. Jesus Christ was Aryan, and the Jews had killed Jesus Christ.

The foundational text for this brand of Christianity was taken from Romans 13, the Apostle Paul's admonition to respect authority, grossly taken out of context and further corrupted when the state authority of the day replaced justice with Nazi ideology. An ideological religion that is in denial about sin and thinks of itself as positive and being full of itself has only one place to go, to the place of hate—hatred of objective thinking, hatred of critical thinking, hatred of the Jew, hatred of the Christian, hatred of the Covenant, hatred of God.

Nowhere in the world are the abuse of mercy and the contempt of God and this double standard more apparent than in the Israeli-Palestinian conflict. The entire world is focused on Israel, requiring the Jew to subscribe to the highest standard of integrity (mercy), which is really a cover for the ideological worlds' intended requirement for suicide, whereas Palestinians and most of the rest of the world may hate and kill with impunity.

We do not return evil with evil for the exact reason that we do not approve of evil; and neither can Justice have over- reach or under-reach; the penalty will be proportionate to the crime.

Justice is self-defence. Without the right to self-defence there is no justice. This is biblical and logical. We will continue to defend justice, and we will have a solution to hate in justice. We will continue to wait and defend ourselves. It is up to the haters to decide how justice will be achieved. Your hate can be thrown out. It's called repentance and coming to your senses.

4

RACISM

I am a conservative. In the contemporary environment of identity politics, and in the opinion of the ideological liberal elite and academia, that means I am a bigot and a racist. That is what they have called us for years. Let me show you how racist I am.

I am an immigrant belonging to a minority group, if there should be such a thing as putting people into identity boxes. I came to Canada with my parents in 1960 from the Netherlands, and because of this, I am known as Dutch. It is my surname that betrays me and gives me that identity.

It was the night of October 31, 1960, that we arrived at Toronto International Airport. At that time jet travel was still new. We were picked up at the airport by our sponsors, who drove us to our new home north of Guelph. On our drive, which was around midnight, the driver had to swerve around a stack of burning straw bales in the middle of the road. Apparently this was a Halloween prank, and it was our first impression of Canada. Halloween was unknown to us. For us October 31 is Reformation Day, when we have a special observance marking the beginning of the Protestant Reformation.

In order to qualify for immigration, since our family had no money, my dad had to fulfill one year of labour on a farm, which was our first destination on arrival. At that time we were the exotic people in the community. We soon learned the language and how to make deals. We quickly found ways to buy property and farms. We Dutch immigrants soon became a community of successful farmers, contractors, and businesspeople. Were we subject to discrimination? We, like all conservatives, often experienced envy and contempt from people in the community, in particular from the ideological left. For us, it is often cast in terms of "you Dutch," a term used to describe our business success, our work ethic, and our Dutch Reformed Calvinist faith.

There is a reserved contempt, even hate, from the ideological liberal left towards our community. It is most apparent in their opposition to our private Christian schools. In our schools, our children are out of reach of the public school and its ideological indoctrination. We teach the Covenant as it is from the Bible, including the biblical requirement to be objective concerning creation and reality. We teach a confidence in reality. We do not teach ideology or alternative realities that are biased and idolatrous. We are also getting better at teaching an objective defence of the Bible.

Today I believe the Christian schools are more secular or civil than the public schools. The common grace of the biblical Covenant is the same common grace of civil life. The covenantal requirement to be objective concerning creation and reality applies to religious life as well as to civil or secular life; there is no difference. At one time we all knew this. It's very ironic that in Ontario, Canada, we get to choose our school support on our property tax assessments. The choice is Roman Catholic or Protestant, and "Protestant" refers only to the public schools (the most current wording used on the assessment form is "Catholic Education or Public"). We choose Protestant, and what we get are ideological and pagan indoctrinations, an identity politics in our public schools that create confusion, derision, and dependency for the justification of a greater tyranny of more state involvement and state overreach. This veiled or not-so-veiled hate and discrimination towards us for these reasons is no different from anti-Semitism.

Before we continue, I think we should consider the meaning of the word "secular" and find a good definition for it before we become confused. I use the word often in this book but always in its objective meaning. The word "secular" does not mean the same thing to everyone because it's not possible to be truly secular in the sense we hope or suppose it would be. The most current definition for the word "secular" provided on a Google search is, "denoting attitudes, activities or other things that have no religious or spiritual basis." This definition explains nothing; it leaves us asking the question, on what basis? With the logical mind, nothing is baseless. Then logically, if it is not to be religious or spiritual, we would be looking for a base of non-conflict between people and their institutions. There is only one thing left to appeal to, which is objective reality to the exclusion of alterative motives and alternate realities.

It is for this purpose we have been given the biblical Covenant and moral law so that we might be objective concerning creation and reality and be stewards of life in the context of creation, reality, and equality of justice. This is our Judaeo-Christian heritage of Western states that support the separation of church and state. The separation of church and state is not a separation of God and reality. It should actually be a confirmation of God and reality both in state and church.

Historically, it is the abuse and tyranny of alterative motives in the church and state we are trying to prevent or overcome. Reality explains itself in light of the Covenant and its justice—the framework or parameters for knowledge a priori. It does not need an interpretation from ideology or any tyranny. It is in this sense that I believe, as I mentioned previously, Christian schools are more secular than public schools. They are more objective concerning reality, (we follow the science not the ideology).

Once the state begins entertaining ideology and alternate realities in the public forum, the state becomes a religious institution mandating non-objective or ideological observances and faith, and the separation between church and state is lost. The notion of being secular is also lost. *Webster's Dictionary* defines "secular" as, "relating to the world, temporal, not ecclesiastical or clerical, not bound by monastic vows or rules, not belonging to a religious order; concerned with temporal worldly matters rather than with religion; having no religious, sacred or spiritual aspect; existing or continuing through centuries and ages." The word "secular" was used in Christian Latin to mean "the world." Replacing one religion with another or one ideology with another, such as secularism, is not secular.

Now apart from all this, what do I think about skin colour and race? In some small way, I grew up with African Jamaican being a part of our family. I said earlier that I worked on the family farm, and we needed many seasonal workers for our orchards, strawberry fields, and tree nursery. We hired local help, including students in the summer during the school break. We also hired many moms who came to work after the children were off to school and left work before the children got home. This worked very well for us. In addition to these workers, we had a crew of offshore migrant workers from Jamaica. In time, I became their boss and liaison. I loved these guys; they were like brothers to me. Being migrant workers, they lived on the farm and were with us twenty-four hours a day. They were available to work longer hours but also for social time together. They and their culture were part of our family.

For the purpose of this book, I make one observation concerning these migrant workers. Culturally, we are a Calvinist-Puritan family. We keep the Sabbath, and for us that is Sunday. We do not work, and nor do our employees. Our business is closed for the day. Whether it is planting time or harvest, we keep the Sabbath. We attend church twice on Sundays, morning and evening. It's our opinion that if you can't make a living in six days, you won't make it in seven days either.

Our resident labourers also got the Sabbath day off. We do not give them a list of things to do while we sit in church; we invite them to come with us to church. We extend the same values to them as to one of us, and some accept the invitation. The others get to rest and socialize on the farm or take a bicycle uptown. If any of them wants to work on Sunday, our answer was that they might work longer hours during the work week. And if that were not agreeable, if they could not adhere to our policy, they did not have to accept the invitation to work on our farm. However, it never was an issue; they were always happy to come back year after year.

Now you might realize my invitation split these workers into two groups. However, the division has always been there. It's not between those who will go with me to my church and those who don't. There is a bigger divide. One group is made up of men who are married and support a wife and children back in Jamaica. These men belong to a Christian community. They usually don't smoke and don't buy lottery tickets. They are positive in outlook and mostly happy. The other group are not married but have a girlfriend in this town and another in another town, a child with this woman and another with that woman, and not necessarily with the current girlfriend. They usually smoke and buy lottery tickets as if that's their religion. They are mostly out of money and quite often not so happy.

What makes the difference? It's obviously not race. When we make race equal to behaviour and social values, as identity politics does, it is a new low and a very evil work. So now when I criticize the behaviour of someone of colour, I can be called racist. However, by the same logic, the ideologist has cover for his or her own promiscuity, immorality, and ideological fantasies. All objectiveness is removed and lost. All criticism is met with claims of racism and bigotry. This is evolutionism and social Darwinism all over again but in reverse. Rather than using race tied to behaviour to prove a race is inferior, they are now are using their own immoral behaviour tied to and equalized with race to prove there should be no moral standards. This modern liberal ideology has no more value for the African American than to be the equivalency of the immoral values the ideology promotes. You are useful as long as you can be weaponized for their ideology.

However, it is clear that the real difference is one of values concerning relationships and the confidence in ourselves concerning these values. The one group is covenantal whereas the other ideological; I think primarily to avoid responsibility. In my opinion, they have not gown up and matured in knowledge to resist the temptations provided by an ideological influence. This has nothing to do with race. Everyone is affected by this influence, and anyone can be vulnerable.

Today our family is a mixed-race family. I have an African-Canadian-Jamaican son-in-law and beautiful mixed-race grandsons. Our recognizable family heritage as Canadians is Dutch Calvinist but includes Jewish and French Huguenot. Now our grandsons can also add African-Jamaican, Nothing of the Covenant is lost on race or skin colour. We are a family and nation of the Covenant, not a race. We are descendants of our ancestors and not trying to be clones.

We are the descendants from the persecuted people of Europe. Our ancestors were persecuted for their faith and the Covenant, which is also the only foundation for constitutional government and human rights. It is for all of this that they were tortured, burned at the stake, or just killed by the Spanish Inquisition and in the religious wars of Europe. Today we are again looking at the same tyranny, the same ideological elite as before who destroy the common grace and repress and forbid knowledge because they think they hold the truth.

The logical solution for racism and all discrimination is the Covenant, the rule of God, the unalienable rights of Man founded in and on the rule of God: "I will be your God, you will be my people". It's called humility; humility toward our Creator, and therefore, it is objective in its application. Racism should never have occurred. Like the Covenant, there is really only one race, the Human Race.

5

THE TESTS

So is there a test for the social contract, identity politics, and political correctness? And where is modern liberal identity politics and political correctness going to lead us? If these are successful; we will be back in the very same Dark Age where we have been before. In this chapter I compare the biblical Covenant to the ideological social contract. You need to remember what I am writing here is social-political philosophy based on logic in the context of the Covenant for you to debate. It is not intended to be theology. I compare the values and the conduct within the biblical Covenant with those of the social contract as discovered from history concerning the following topics: slavery, human sacrifice vs. human rights, the common or civil Grace, the law, and subjective faith.

Slavery in the Bible

When slavery occurred in the Bible's account of history it was in payment of a debt or involved prisoners of war. However, under the Covenant, slaves were to be made free in time, and could become citizens, and Jews. Slavery was never hereditary or racist.

Human Sacrifice

In the Bible we read that God called Abraham from Ur of the Chaldees in Mesopotamia and promised him that he would become a nation, and in him all the families of the earth would be blessed. God called Abraham to be a reformer in his time. God tried Abraham on his faith by asking him to sacrifice his only son, the son of the Covenant promise. To do so would be in keeping with the extreme piety that existed in the religion of his time. When his son Isaac asked, "But where is the lamb for a burnt offering?" (Genesis 22:7,8 AKJV), Abraham answered that God would provide. And God did provide; Isaac was not sacrificed. This was the end of human sacrifice and the beginning of human rights for the nation of Israel, and by extension, to the world. God Himself would provide for righteousness in Justice for his people. God proved to Abraham and all of his descendants and us that God is the God He said He is and not, as some pagan god. Human rights can only begin when we ban human sacrifice. You may read this in more detail in Genesis 22.

Later, when Israel received the Promised Land, the Bible states that the heathens were cast out of the land because they sacrificed their children to Moloch and worshipped Baal and Ashtoreth. Heathens were not driven out because Israel was made up of such good and deserving people. The children of Israel were also told if they did these abominable things, they would also be cast out of this land they had been promised.

The Covenant of Grace

According to the Bible, there is only one Covenant, the Covenant of grace that began after the fall of man (humankind) and the beginning of sin. The first indication of this Covenant we get from the Bible can be found in the book of Genesis, where God calls Adam, "Where art thou?" (Genesis 3:9 AVJK). At this time

Satan was cursed and Eve was promised the coming Messiah. The Covenant is God reaching out for us to be objective about what we have done, what we are, and then how we are to be restored. It is the beginning of a common grace leading to saving grace; all other covenants mentioned in the Bible are in the context of this Covenant of God's grace.

The Moral Law or the Ten Commandments

The moral law was received and given by Moses prior to the children of Israel entering the Promised Land. It became the constitution for the children of Israel as nation, kingdom, and state. This law is for both religious and secular or civil life. It was given to sinners for their own good. The benefit and blessing of the law is inherent in the law itself; this should be self-evident. The experience from this law for the sinner should be to improve life through an objective understanding of human relationships and humility- the mercy of God - leading us to repentance, salvation, and restoration to the Covenant and to God.

Again we discover a common grace in the moral law that is general to everyone and to everyone's benefit. The moral law is grace; the requirement to be objective is grace. All of this is grace in a common or secular life. Then there is also saving grace that is particular and spiritual, a subjective faith in confirmation of the Covenant and its moral law with an applied salvation from God. This faith can never be legislated into law by any government; it is the gift from God. However, the common grace provided for by the moral law is for everyone and must be observed as the rule of law regardless of faith for everyone's benefit. It is the objective law for civil society that makes cooperation and progress possible.

Moral law did not begin with Moses. These concepts were known and should have been known since the beginning. With Moses they became written as a constitution, the moral code for a nation and the government of that nation. It is noteworthy that it was only the Ten Commandments that were placed in the Ark of the Covenant, not the entire Torah. It is all every person needs to know to be a moral person and discover the need for repentance and salvation. The greatest social benefit realized from the moral law is in the supremacy of God, allowing God to be God, and that we would be objective concerning creation and reality, which should therefore also be reflected in the entire rule of law; the only sustainable common peace; our responsibility that makes us free.

Subjective Faith and Saving Faith

Faith in Jesus Christ as our Saviour from sin, provider of our righteousness is a spiritual matter given to us as individuals from God. It is all out of reach of government but nevertheless of great value to society and the government by its reciprocal confirmation of the Covenant, moral law, and self governance of the citizen. In this regard, ideological Christianity, which preaches Christ out of context, has done a lot of harm to society and the credibility of the church. If the church denies common grace and the moral law as grace and essential to saving grace, then there would be no sin. Christ becomes a pagan sacrifice, and the forgiveness of sin becomes the approval of sin. The reciprocity of the Covenant is broken or denied. This is why your churches are empty and closing. In the Bible, Jude writes of this, "turning the grace of our God into lasciviousness" (Jude 1:4 AKJV).

To be understood correctly, Jesus Christ is the Saviour from sin in the context of the Covenant, the moral law, and God's justice. This has been provided for by God. It is not some pagan sacrifice of a human being bringing another human being to be sacrificed to the gods for some special favour or benefit. That would be an abomination.

Christ then is preached in the context of the Covenant, the

moral law, and repentance. Once having received Christ, you would want to keep the law; it should be in our hearts. Our desire to do and our righteousness is Christ and Christ alone. Christ paid the price for sin in God's justice. Again, all of this is received in faith, not by any law of the State. This realization should be logical to everyone.

Allow me to write one more thing concerning Jesus Christ as our Saviour from sin in the context of God's justice. It is also relevant to understanding the limitations of the civil or secular state. In the time of the Old Testament, the gate of any city was also the seat of justice, the court. When the Bible refers to Zion's gate, it is symbolic for the seat of God's justice. It was in this court that the Jews accused Jesus Christ of making Himself equal to God; and as no man is God, they condemned Him to death. If Jesus is to be a Saviour for our sin, then this is the right accusation. The apex and embodiment of all our sins is that we try to be our own god. He had to be accused of our sins; we all are in the same condemnation. (Well then so much for a history of calling the Jews the Christ-killers.) At the time of the crucifixion, Christ's disciples left Him also. Isaiah prophesised of this: "I have trodden the wine press alone; and of the people there was none with me" (Isaiah 63 AKJV). Salvation is the work of God alone.

The accusation that no man is God is very right; the created cannot simultaneously be the creator. But do we put that limitation on God? Should we not allow God to be God, the eternal King of Zion? Christ who said, "Forgive them for they know not what they do" (Luke 23:34 AKJV), and to His disciples, "I have prayed for you that your faith fail not" (Luke 22:32 AKJV). Then we read in Psalm 118 AKJV, "The stone which the builders refused is become the head stone of the corner. This is the Lords doing; it is marvellous in our eyes. Open to me the gates of righteousness and I will enter them with praise."

All of this again is received in faith, reaching forward to the day we apprehend. Again no government can legislate this faith into law. But the state under the Covenant is required to enforce the Convent rule of law to establish a common grace, which is also the civil and secular grace for every citizen. At the same time, it is also the context for the gospel and the foundation for freedom, objective human rights, and making democracy possible for a civil society.

Now I shall do the same analysis for ideology and its imitation of the Covenant, the social contract.

Slavery

I have said earlier that slavery was for the payment of a debt and an option for prisoners of war. Obviously and historically slavery is for an economic advantage—cheap labour and cheap consumer goods. When there is a shortage of money in an economy, you can sell insolvent people into slavery. This has worked as a form of austerity throughout history. It works effectively by eliminating participants in the moneyed economy but still keeping them as productive participants in the economy. (Today so-called sweatshops are used in totalitarian and communist states to achieve the same advantage).

Now the next question is what can we do with prisoners of war? Historically what happened? You could just kill them. You could sacrifice them to the gods and make a sacrament out of it. Then you could also take them as lifelong slaves. You could also return them or send them away as refugees, which rarely happened.

The notion of hereditary racist slavery in western states is a modern invention that began in the seventeenth century and has evolved over centuries. It included buying captured prisoners of war from Africa (well, supposedly prisoners of war) and then selling them to the colonies to provide labour. If they were truly treated as prisoners of war, then after a time, they would be freed and given citizenship. At the least, the slavery would not extend to the next generation. This did not happen. Instead, a system of racism and dependency developed. Economic necessity and greed developed into an economic and social ideology to defend racism and racist slavery.

The ideology divided nations and the church. Unfortunately, many Christian churches are ideological rather than biblical. They seeking acceptance in popular ideology rather than teaching and defending the biblical Covenant and the Gospels. This ideology was reinforced with later ideologies, such as Utilitarianism, Evolutionism, Social Darwinism, Nietzscheism and Nazism. Despite the resistance to slavery by countless Christians over centuries, racism persisted long after the Civil War freed the slaves in the United States. It is based on the power of these later ideologies that so many of us have been able to remain racist.

Human Sacrifice

I began this book by describing the human sacrifices of the Mayan, Aztecs, and Inca of the Americas, the Mayan in particular. Human sacrifice appears to have been a part of all or most primitive religions and cultures around the world. I believe there must be some compelling but tragic spiritual need. I think it may come from our realization of our smallness and a lack of knowledge combined with fear, guilt, and alienation. Whatever the cause, it existed. Obviously, a feeling of comfort for oneself is always sought.

In the Mediterranean region at the about the time of the original founding of the nation of Israel, the prevailing pagan religions practiced infanticide as human sacrifice. A baby, usually a newborn, was roasted to death on a fire inside a hollow statue of the god Moloch.

Were these human sacrifices brought only out of piety to please the gods and invoke favour, or were they also as a means of disposing unwanted children, who were made into a sacrifice as some good deed to appease the guilt for the murder? We will never know the extent of either, but I think it was a combination of both.

What are we doing today? For a long time the pro-choice argument was that the unborn child is not a human being but just a fetus, just the product of conception, some nonhuman thing and, therefore, could have no recognition as a human being, so the idea of human rights was absurd. This argument has been demolished by science. It was an attempt to write myth, fantasy, and falsehood into law, as well as enforce the faith in this delusion as the rule of law.

Today in Canada we have no abortion law at all; abortion is legal up until birth. In the United States, there are also attempts by some states to make it legal up until birth. The ideology approves of infanticide; there is no shame. You may kill your child for any greater good. Currently on social media there is a hashtag circulating, "#shout your abortion." They unknowingly are making infanticide into a sacrament. That is the only outcome possible from their actions, a sacrifice to the god of self-identification, the religion of consumerism and environmentalism and climate religion, like paganism. It could be anything.

This one sacrament is the end for all human rights. You need to think critically. Infanticide is discrimination without regard for humanity. The human being becomes the property of the tyrant for him or her to do with as they want. This discrimination is now a required article of faith for everyone. All society is to be brought into the servitude of this religion. It becomes intellectual slavery—mandatory state religion—and when you do not share the faith, you are excluded from the state; you may no longer participate in the state.

Then we also have the ideological right to die. Medically assisted dying, the right to suicide, the choice for death also becomes a sacrament, taking away shame and guilt. However we have just removed all human rights with the practice of infanticide. Medically assisted dying will soon become medically assisted execution of the unwanted. It is inherent in the ideology. You are now challenged to prove that it is not. Do you really think you can maintain a double standard? Of course the ideology can give us better heath care, and free healthcare; they just kill more people. With the right to kill, all objectiveness is lost.

Common and Civil Grace

In modern ideology anything that might be considered to resemble a substitute for grace is moral relativism, tolerance of self-destruction, and our neighbor and community as well.

I said earlier that the moral law, the Ten Commandments from the Bible, are grace and essential for grace and are as much secular and civil as religious. The ideological left, with all its political correctness, has all but banned this moral law from any appearance in the public sphere, dismissing it as religion and having no place in the secular state. If you really think it has no place in the public forum and no force of law for secular life, you need to write the opposite of it and try to enforce that as the rule of law. Then see what you get. To a large degree that is what the ideological left is doing because that is what moral relativism is. We become a merciless society.

The attack on biblical moral law from moral relativism is really a denial of the rule of law in its totality. They replace it with policy, ideological policy that is arbitrary, contradictory, and self-refuting. All of this doesn't matter; ideology is served as justice.

We have just seen a great display of this type of justice in the United States by the Congress in its impeachment of the president, Donald Trump. Granted, Congress is not a court of justice. Nevertheless, it was very revealing to see what ideological justice looks like. It reminded me of Stalinist Soviet justice: "show me the man and I'll show you the crime." It is this Soviet ideological justice that sent more than 20 million of their own people to their deaths in the gulag. You need to know your history. You need to read Aleksandr Solzhenitsyn's book *The Gulag Archipelago*. It begins with the arrest, interrogation, fabrication of evidence, and the repression of truth. The concentration camp begins in the courthouse, even Congress when ideology takes over.

What we are seeing here is the progression of political correctness and wokeness revealing itself as a Marxist culture and replacement justice from the academia. In the United States and most Western democracies, economic Marxism was unable to get established because these states have a large middle class that owns property; they share in the wealth of the nation and the land. We won't give up our property for collectivism. However, culture and justice do not have material property; they are intellectual property. It is this property that is being expropriated from us now and replaced with a constructed reality. Then it follows that crime will also become a constructed reality.

We no longer have any idea of what we might be guilty; To achieve major convictions, crimes are being fabricated and constructed out of alternate realities and pettiness. No one is safe any longer under this Marxist ideological alternate reality for justice. It no longer is justice. Instead we have an ideological system intentionally designed to demoralize and destroy people.

Today, wherever western Marxist replacement justice is taking hold, it is a crime to participate in aspects of our intellectual property and rights, such as freedom of conscience, academic freedom, objective thinking, and critical thinking. Each of these can now get you arrested.

In all of this, where is the public good? The public good has become nihilism. What the ideology wants from us is a dysfunctional confusion of self-identification and to be detached from reality, all for the benefit of the ideological elite. We need to be demoralized and deconstructed. All of this is also the deconstruction of the Covenant. How is any of this useful for the ideological liberal billionaires but also socialist, communists, the elite that espouse these values? As I see it, they—the progressive academia—are trying to construct a nihilist world order. This requires the destruction of the free West through the expropriation of our intellectual property (our rights) and after that, our physical and economic properties. Yes, such is the substitute for common grace, civil grace, from ideology.

Spirituality

Does moral relativism have any spirituality and faith? As I have just mentioned, beginning with abortion, it requires non-thinking faith to believe that the unborn is not a human being. To live like that requires living a make-believe existence. For many of us, that is hard to do. Now today, in the year 2021 we are required to believe that we can or should kill any unwanted child for any perceived superior benefit. The value of the child ends in a sacrament. Again am I required to have that faith, a religion where life has no value, where there is no sin, but people are pollution, and we dispose of the unwanted?

When life has no value or purpose other than that defined by the elite, then life becomes the creations of the elite. Hence we now have the newly constructed subspecies of human being requiring an alternate host in order to reproduce. Yes, a handsome addition to elitism, one that can also be weaponized for persecution. Then we also have the introduction of sexual discrimination against the opposite sex as a matter of public policy and an article of faith. And yes, we must keep the faith. It is mandatory.

Yes, except if you wholly keep the faith, you cannot be a citizen of the state. You may not be a teacher, lawyer, doctor, marriage commissioner, judge, or hold any public office because you are of the wrong religion. Anyone attempting to apply for public office or public employment will be given a litmus test to discover faithfulness to the right religion. This has become the religious inquisition of the twenty-first century. Of course supporters of pro-life and pro-family are religious heretics. Critical thinking and objective thinking have become crimes.

The ideological judges on the courts, including the supreme

courts, become—or are—ideological high priests divining state religion. Justice is turned into pragmatic ideological policy of Marxism. There is no justice in an ideological state. None; In the United States we have seen the trend of ideologically motivated judgements to give the maximum penalties. If we don't stop it, it will become the gulag of western Marxism.

In this modern Western, liberal, Marxist, pagan ideological social contract, there is no room for the people of the Covenant, the nation of the Covenant. The ideology is a replacement religion, a pagan absolutism with five articles of mandatory faith—the rights to abortion, infanticide, eugenics, ethnic cleansing, and genocide— because people are not sinners but pollution. They will save the earth by these five rights. Anti-Semitism again becomes a sacrament, and this time there is no difference between the Jew and Christian. It is the Covenant and the Constitution of the State that have to go.

It is a quasi-social-environmental-climate religion that has brought back the pagan sacrifice. It is about offsetting their carbon foot print by doing something good for the environment. Like sacrificing you and paying support to dictators for eliminating unwanted populations- it's just a cultural thing. The United States and the west need to become such totalitarianism. No one is going to stop flying their private jets, no – instead more people will be flying in private jets, it's you that will not be traveling.

This ideology can only lead to another holocaust. It is the inherent nature of this ideology.

Test Conclusion

We need a major repentance and return to the Covenant, the supremacy of God, and the rule of law. Where the first truth is God exists and is not man. And the greatest lie is that man created himself. It is the difference between reality and fantasy, order and chaos, stewardship and nihilism.

Regardless of this, the nation of the Covenant needs to wake up, open its eyes, and not walk blindly; believing things are not really that bad. We should not pretend to go with the flow as a long-term protection, believing we will escape. Many of us did that before the last Holocaust until it was too late. We should not repeat that. Pretending to go with the flow may work as a short-term strategy to achieve particular victory in certain critical circumstances, but not for survival.

> First they came for the socialist and I did not speak out—because I was not a socialist.

> Then they came for the trade unionist and I did not speak our—because I was not a trade unionist.

> Then they came for the Jew and I did not speak out—because I was not a Jew.

> Then they came for me—and there was no one left to speak for me. (Niemoller)

> Niemoller, who wrote this poem, was a German Lutheran pastor who originally was a Nazi supporter during its rise to power. He soon came to realize his cowardice and that of the German intellectuals who all became victims of it.

Today's threat in the west and the world, again, is not about socialist, trade unions, Jews, or anything else; it is the covenantal right to have life and to have a conscience at all.

We need to defend ourselves in the entire world and engage our enemy with no uncertain terms. We need to call things out for what they are at every level in society and government.

We need to take back the secular, civil state from social and judicial Marxism, and put the state back on the base of the Constitution, the Covenant, and the supremacy of God and the rule of law, on objective reality. We must never accept ideology and its reconstruction of the Constitution into manifestos of alternate realities and its fake justice. The ideology of secularism is not secular. That term has been used as a transition for the secular state to move into an ideological pagan state. We have an inalienable right to be free from ideology and its tyranny.

We will have the right to life. We will have pro-life health care and pro-life hospitals. We will have academic freedom. We will have schools free from ideology. Ideology can have no governance over academic freedom; it is a contradiction. We will have parental choice of schools.

We need to fight for all these things and become the majority in our own country. Even when we are not the majority, we still have the right to all of this because we are equal citizens. This also includes the rights of all citizens to hold public office. We are witnesses for truth and its reality in the world, we do not back down but work together and support each other.

Let Me Explain a Few Terms

What is ideological tyranny, and why does it so often produce a murderous tyrant as is evident from the world's history? It is a mandatory state religion of elitism, human discrimination, and sacrifice. You might not think this is religion, but that is what it is. People are more religious than we want to believe. People believe it as popular culture. This works towards the elimination of objective realty in favour of relativism to accommodate the ideology and its alternate realities. In the end, nihilism reigns supreme.

Why are they so murderous? All ideology proves one important fact: Proponents of it cannot deal with human sin. Not their own or another's. They know no forgiveness for they have no sin, everything is relative; nevertheless, they are always right. They inhale and are terrified to exhale; they might lose it all. They require your help as a catastrophe is imminent, and you must grab yourself an alternate reality to save yourself and the planet. Eventually the reality of alternate reality drives all of them to derangement. Then one deranged leader stands up and kills them all; at least all those who were wrong. This is the reciprocity of the social contract.

To say it in another way, ideological relativism and the alternate realities would like to freeze the entire world so that not a snowflake would melt. In this way they can freeze out the guilt of sin.

What is sin? Now that I have used the word "sin," I should explain what it is for those who might not know. In relativism, there can be no sin as all things are only relative. But then to say anything is objective would be wrong, a sin. An alternate reality is actually saying that reality is sin. This is their derangement, and reality will be punished for it.

In the Hebrew Bible, sin simply means to miss the mark. For a mark to exist requires a reality that is objective a priori. That reality is the moral law: to love God above all and our neighbours as ourselves. This is the requirement of being objective concerning the reality of all creation, including the self. For the state that is the supremacy of God and the rule of law, I will be your God; you will be my people, which is the foundation of constitutional government and our defence against encroaching ideological tyranny.

In the Bible, Genesis 17, 7 (AKJV) we read about Abraham a father of many nations and the Chosen Israel .... "An everlasting covenant, to be a God unto thee and to thy seed after thee.....and I will be their God". From this text you might theologically challenge me for using it as a universal Covenant and not just limited to the Jews. To be Jewish, of this particular Covenant, is leadership in the Covenant of Grace toward the work of salvation, the original covenant with Adam. It is not elitism. The entire Biblical message from the Old Testament and New Testament make that clear.

We need a major repentance returning to the Covenant. Yes, repentance is also logical. You need to come to yourself when you remember or learn the Covenant. You might even find the Saviour. "Ask and you will receive, seek and you will find, knock and it will be opened to you" (Mathew 7:7 AKJV). This is a quote from the Bible encouraging you to use the means of grace.

A street scene in the Old City of Jerusalem.

The western wall of the Temple Mount at Jerusalem, where we come to pray.

While visiting with Palestinian Arabs in the East Quarter of Old Jerusalem this is as close I could come to the Dome of the Rock, I was not allowed to enter this gate since I am not Moslem.

With Ethiopian Jews in Israel.

*On the rooftops of old City Jerusalem, a different
view - but like my book very real and true.*

*One of the may stone alters on the pyramids at the Mayan city of
Chichin Itza Mexico upon which was place the offering of a pulsating
human heart to the gods that was cut out of the chest of a live human
sacrifice. It should remind us of what kind of people do we want
to be? Do we want the covenant? Or do we want Ideology?*

6

HOW IS ISRAEL A JEWISH STATE?

This chapter discusses some important questions about Israel and being Jewish. What makes Israel a Jewish state? Can Israel be a Jewish state without being a state of discrimination? What is Jewish identity? The Covenant is our identity, nothing more, nothing less, lived and confirmed by a moral cultural lifestyle. To be sure it is not secularism or Judaism. An ideological interpretation of what is secular is not secular; nor is it the content of the Covenant. So neither an ideological interpretation of the Torah and scriptures is either Jewish or the Covenant. We should let the primary Covenant speak for itself as it is found in scripture to be our identity. Much of the ancient ceremonial and cultural laws cannot be kept in our time, and I don't think they are primary to the Covenant but of value in their concepts confirming the Covenant.

Then it follows that a Jewish state is also a constitutional state based on the Covenant - again nothing more and nothing less. The biblical Covenant is, and has been demonstrated to be, the only inalienable foundation for real human rights and constitutional government. In this regard, the Jewish state should be a model state for the world.

Language, culture, and faith become the reinforcement of this Covenant, and its moral law becomes a self-governing constitution for the family nation and state. The state will only benefit from faith when the people have reason to believe that the state upholds the Covenant.

The threats to the Jewish state are no different than the threat to any Covenant or constitutional state that values human rights. Only for Israel they have been much more intense because of armed hostility supported by an international hostile world view—or maybe it's a God view. The enemies of the Jewish state are also the enemies of the Covenant. They are ideologies, alternate realities, and tyrannies; it is all idolatry. Jews and Gentiles are as much susceptible to ideology as those we see as our enemies. We need to stop embracing Covenant-hating ideologies in our personal lives and as a nation and state. We need to stop persecuting each other on issues of faith and embrace the Covenant for its objective reality and value.

Historically, who are the Jew's and Israel's friends and supporters? They have been very few, but there are some. For example, from the first century BC and AD there is evidence that many Greeks were keeping Sabbath, attending synagogues, and studying the Torah; at that time the Hebrew Scriptures were available in the Greek language, the "Septuagint." There was an interest in Jewish religion. The pagan Greek-Roman religions were in disrepute and decline. People were getting tired of the sexualized paganism. These Greeks soon became Christian, which at that time was considered a Jewish sect. These Greek-Jewish believers were sometimes called atheists because they rejected the pagan gods; something like being called a deplorable today! It is clear that Jewish support came from Gentiles embracing the Covenant.

After this we have a long history of Roman Catholic and Greek Orthodox anti-Semitism and periodic intermittent persecutions along with the development of a mutual animosity between the rabbis and the pope. This persecution in Western Europe continued, interrupted only by the Protestant Reformation, and then only by some reformers.

The reformation was a return to the Bible, the Covenant of the Bible, for the rule of life, faith, salvation, religion, and government. The Reformation was also a total rejection of the ideological tyranny concerning religion mandated by the Roman Catholic Church at that time. The Protestant Netherlands gained their independence from Spain through a war that lasted from 1581 to 1648, ending with the treaty of Westphalia. Finally we were rid of the Roman Catholic Spanish inquisition, tyranny, and persecution; it was free to take in refugees from the same persecution. Many Sephardic Jews from Spain went to the Netherlands and made it their new home. The House of Orange, the Dutch prince, became their protector.

Why was the Dutch Calvinist Reformation so favorable to the emancipation of the Jews? It is not that Jews are such special people; we treat them the same as our own. Rather, that is what emancipation is about, but more so for the Covenant. We have the Covenant of grace through the Bible and by the Covenant with Abraham and Israel. When you can see the gospel in the context of this Covenant, all you can do is emancipate the Jews. But then you would also do this for all people who seek this freedom to live by the Covenant. We see ourselves in the same Covenant of grace but as Gentiles and not specific to the Promised Land and the nation of Israel. The biggest problem with emancipation for the Jews was assimilation, but then that is an internal problem with the religion of Judaism and identity, not with emancipation or the Covenant.

This same emancipation took hold in England with Oliver Cromwell's republic. He invited the Jews back to England. The Puritans of Great Britain were of the same opinion as the Dutch Reformed about the Jews and the Covenant. This Protestant, Puritan, and Calvinist return to the Bible and defence of the Covenant also went to North America. There, in time, it became the constitutional government of the new state, the United States of America. To a large degree, it is the Protestant Reformation, the return to the Biblical Covenant, along with the emancipation of the Jews and all people that made Western democracies possible.

Now compare this with the Jewish emancipation in Germany. Napoleon invaded, conquered the German states, and forcibly emancipated the Jews against the wishes of the German elites. This was not an emancipation founded on a faith, for the love of God and the Covenant, but rather a social contract that needed a lot of work. This social contract ended 130 years later in the Holocaust.

Napoleon also invaded the Netherlands in 1797, deposed the House of Orange, and established the Batavian Republic in the Netherlands, which lasted until 1805. Did Napoleon come to emancipate the Jews? The Jews had already been emancipated in the Netherlands for more than 150 years; the now-deposed House of Orange had been their protector. Napoleon was not so helpful in the Netherlands. His reasons were conquest, not the Covenant or any lasting benefit for the Jews.

It is through the love for the Covenant and ultimately God that we can achieve much. We are pro-life, pro-family, and pro-Israel because we defend objective reality against the ideological tyranny of alternate realities. In human rights all people are equal. Remember that the Holocaust was the result of an ideological alternate reality—Nazism. Never again!

Palestinian Refugees

Are they still refugees? To date, every proposal for a Palestinian state has been refused. The intent to eliminate the Jews and Israel from of the earth is being taught in Palestinian schools and reaffirmed constantly by Palestinians in their political philosophy and cultural society. The time for a Palestinian state is long past. They should be required to migrate to the states that declared war on Israel on their behalf. That was and still is their logical new home after the war.

These states have greater responsibilities to the Palestinian refugees than Israel does. The world should be funding them to migrate rather than paying them to stay in the occupied Israeli territories. The only possibility for staying in the occupied territories would be the acceptance of the State of Israel and a commitment to all equality in everything pertaining to objective human rights in civil life; In other words, the Covenant for its secular value, its common grace, but without needing to be Jewish or Christian.

But then we remember if there was no Covenant, there would be no Jews. So what do they want?

I will tell you what they want. They want the same thing as Western ideological alternate realities appear to be achieving in the Western states: the elimination of the Covenant, the supremacy of God, and the rule of law; and along with it all human rights to eliminate the Jew and Christian. As long as the ideological alternate realities in the Western states are gaining power, they believe they will get their way and have the state of Israel and the Jew eliminated from the face of the earth. It is objective reality and human rights—the Covenant—that is their common enemy. But it goes deeper. It is actually God.

Israel's Safety

The State of Israel now has some Islamic states as allies. Though that is nice to hear, it is because they have a common enemy, the elite of Iran. When we have allies because we are faced with a mutual enemy that does not mean we have solved any of the problems that existed before the alliance.

If the Jews and Israel are looking for peace, especially a lasting peace, it is in the Covenant. History shows that those people brought into the influence of the biblical Covenant and recognize its requirement to be objective concerning creation and reality become friends and supporters of Israel, ambassadors of goodwill, and the enthusiastic proponents for the emancipation of all people. We need more of these people in the world.

Jews need to become more evangelical with the Covenant as it is the foundation of both religion and secular civil government, a common grace for all. We should leave faith in Jesus Christ to the individual and God. We have seen in what I have argued before in this book that a saving faith can never be forced or legislated. We need to be objective as the covenant requires and not become ideological. You might also want to remember Jews are as much the children of Adam as they are the children of Abraham - and Abraham could only be a son of Adam. Abraham is not replacement theology for Adam – but the continuity of God's redeeming work from the beginning of Adam in the Covenant of Grace to its completion.

We need to reach out with the Covenant to the people of the world, beginning with ourselves. In the past, we in the West have promoted democracy as a solution to every problem in the world and showcasing our own democracy. It has been a failure. Democracy only works with some resemblance of the Covenant.

Then we, Western states and governments, thought globalism and free trade would be the road to peace. Instead we opened the door for global tyranny to inundate the West. Trade only works when it is fair and has some resemblance to the Covenant.

Then we have ideological Western leaders who preach the gospel of moral relativism to the world as if that should bring peace. This is a denial of the covenant by promoting an alternate reality, and results mostly at being laughed at by the world.

When our enemies call us Satan, they may be telling a truth. The Western ideological alternate reality with its moral relativism may appear to be completely at odds with that of our enemy and their ideological alternate reality. But they do have one common enemy, the Covenant. What they are referring to is the same Satan as they have themselves. Their tyranny differs only in how it is expressed.

Peace and progress are achieved through the objective reality afforded and required by the Covenant. "The fear of the Lord is the beginning of wisdom; a good understanding have they that do His Commandments" (Psalm 111:10 AKJV). This scripture has proven to have a lot of relevance in our history as well as today.

Pro-Life

Why do we all, including Jews need to be pro-life? If you truly think you defend human rights, and are against genocide and ethnic cleansing, but support abortion, you need to think again. You also need to be pro-life. You cannot be selective about human life because selectiveness about life is the foundation for genocide and a denial of your own covenant. I will show you.

I will deal with a quote from Henry Morgentaler, a proud quote by which he would like to be remembered. Henry Morgentaler was the Canadian abortionist whose legal efforts led to Canada having no abortion law. Henry Morgentaler is also known as a past president of the Canadian Humanist Association and a self-proclaimed proud womanizer. With all of this, no doubt a Covenant-hating and self-hating Jew.

His statement was, "Every child a wanted child, every mother a willing mother I want to make my contribution to humanity so that there will be no more Auschwitz's. Children who are born wanted and are given love and attention will not build concentration camps." (Last viewed on 2021-01-26 azquotes.com).

You need to make a critical analysis of this statement. You will find that the first sentence is also the foundation for Auschwitz and for all genocide and ethnic cleansing. As it is in the family, so it also is in the state. All you need to do is substitute the word "people" for child and the word "state" for mother: "Every person a wanted person and every state a willing state." Then it follows children born and raised from this elitism definitely will be building concentration camps. You can count on it.

When the love and attention given to these children are the ideological alternate realities from Hollywood and the academia, you can count on it 100 per cent. Concentration camps and all the ideology that goes with and leads to them come from a derangement derived from alternate realities.

Every child is a gift from God, a mother's joy, and the mother, a child's joy. Children nurtured in the love of the Covenant of grace should become men and women of truth and justice, knowing that abortion is not a solution to an inconvenient or unwanted pregnancy. The solution is in our holistic approach towards life as individuals, as a family, and as a community.

The Bible writes numerous times that the children of Israel will be cast out of their land when they serve pagan gods and sacrifice their children to these pagan gods. This still holds true for today. It is not only Israel that will be cast out of its land. The entire West will be cast out and displaced. What I mean is we will lose our democracy and human rights and be servants to repressive ideology in our own countries. We need a major repentance and return to the Covenant.

Concerning concentration camps and Hollywood, if there is a place in this world we need to boycott and disinvest for our own good it is Hollywood and the film industry. They already have built their concentration camps. They are for conservatives and Republicans. They have become a propaganda industry for Social Marxism that attacks with the intent of destroying conservatives. A film industry run by sexual predators, covenant-hating and self-hating Jews and Gentiles is incorporating an ideological agenda of deconstructionism and nihilism to replace the Covenant, or rather, to deconstruct the Covenant in their film products. We need to refuse them.

Abortion-infanticide is never sustainable as a method of population control. In time they will come to realize that the state is full of old people with no one to care for you; before that happens they will switch to eugenics, ethnic cleansing and genocide; kill or sterilizing whole groups of undesirable people.

We see this appears to be happening in communist China. After decades of a one child policy, Chinese government is now detaining Muslims in consecration camps and we hear reports of forced sterilization of these ethnic groups, one of them the Uyghur's, (Aljazeera.com news 01-15-2021 among many others referencing the CECC the Congressional – Executive Commission on China). China calls them re-education camps, vocational training centers to stamp out extremism. We have heard this kind of rhetoric before as a cover for genocide. The Muslims of the world deserve much better; we need to support them in their fight against ethnic cleansing and genocide.

We also recognize that there have been and still are extremist movements and governments among Muslims that advocate ethnic cleansing and genocide, we can now also add to that list the western Marxist- pagan academia as another Ideology, generally supportive of Chinese government and openly advocating re-education in the west targeting the covenantal values held by Christians and Jews including the constitutional values of the State. If we do not stop it, it will lead to no other place but legal ethnic cleansing, genocide, another holocaust.

What is the solution? All of you alarmists who are fearful about the future and the world's population growth, instead of beating up on your neighbour to conform to your fear, you have the freedom to chose sterilization for yourself.

The birth rate and the migration of people might have a chance to stabilize, when we bring people out of poverty and subscribe to real and objective human rights; The Covenant.

7

CONVERSION AND THE CANCEL CULTURE

On the 11th of June 2008, Prime Minister Stephen Harper stood in the House of Commons to offer, on behalf of the Government of Canada, an apology to Aboriginal peoples in Canada for the assimilative policies from government-sanctioned residential schools causing the extensive abuse, suffering and cultural dislocation of individuals their families and communities.

When government partners with ideology, in this case Christian Ideology, Canadians are in trouble, and in this time it was aboriginal or First Nation Canadians. These residential schools began in the 1870s and operated in full force until the 1970s. After this they declined, with the last school closing in 1996.

This was a partnership with organizations from Anglican, Presbyterian, United Church of Canada, the Roman Catholic Church and the Missionary Oblates of Mary Immaculate. All of them have now apologized.

I call this ideological Christianity because there is nothing biblical, covenantal, or gospel about their methods. Rather, their methods, the message, and the purpose are all against the biblical Covenant. How do you engage in an objective discussion about objective truth and reality when you destroy the natural biological family? These residential schools became mandatory and disrupted the family. The biblical Covenant builds on the natural, biological family. It engages parents with their children in discussions concerning objective truth and reality. It does not take children away from the parents to indoctrinate them against their parents or to destroy them through neglect and ideological, intellectual, physical, and sexual abuse.

In Genesis we read, "in thee (Abraham) all of the families of the earth will be blessed" (Genesis 12:3 AKJV). It is through the family that we have success, not by destroying the family. The biological family is the universal and temporal or—secular, or civil —foundation of the Covenant; it is the tangible evidence for the Covenant of grace and builds upon this family. I recognize anti-family ideology as another branch of anti-Semitism. When we destroy the family then the blessing that is in Abraham may have no place to go. This is how the faith of the ideological alternate reality believes, although very oblivious to it.

To be clear, a true missionary believes and knows Indigenous people are as capable of objective thinking and critical thinking as anyone else when given the chance. When you think otherwise it is because you are racist. Mission work is about equality in the Covenant of Grace; it is not radical equity. To mandate a perceived equity in race is apartheid - and it does not matter how you try it interpret it; it always will be apartheid- it will always be for a group and against a group; A racist state of mind, judging people, categorizing people for discrimination, demonization. Think about it!

Now what was the abuse that the government apologized for? Following is the full text of the apology from Hansard No. 110, of June 11, 2008. (39-2) House of Commons of Canada, by copyright permission, 2021-02-15, from the office of the law clerk and Parliamentary Counsel.

Right Hon. Stephen Harper (Prime Minister, CPA)

I stand before you today to offer an apology to former students of Indian Residential schools.

The treatment of children in these schools is a sad chapter in our history.

For more than a century, Indian residential schools separated over 150,000 aboriginal children from their families and communities.

Two primary objectives of the residential school system were to remove and isolate children from the influence of their homes, families, traditions, and culture, and to assimilate them into the dominant culture.

These objectives were based on the assumption that aboriginal culture and spiritual beliefs were inferior and unequal.

Indeed, some sought, as was infamously said, "To kill the Indian in the Indian

Today, we recognize that this policy of assimilation was wrong, has caused great harm, and has no place in our country. One hundred and thirty-two federally supported schools were located in every province and territory, except Newfoundland, New Brunswick and Prince Edward Island.

(Most schools were operated as joint ventures with Anglican, Roman Catholic, Presbyterian, and the United Church.)

The Government of Canada built an educational system in which very young children were often forcibly removed from their homes and often taken far from their communities.

Many were inadequately fed, clothed, and housed. All were deprived of the care and nurturing of their parents, grandparents, and communities.

First Nation, Inuit and Métis languages and cultural practices were prohibited in these schools.

Tragically, some of these children died while attending residential schools and others never returned home.

The government now recognizes that the consequences of the Indian residential schools' policy were profoundly negative and that this policy has had a lasting and damaging impact on aboriginal culture, heritage and language.

While some former students have spoken positively about their experiences at residential schools, these stories are far overshadowed by the tragic accounts of the emotional, physical and sexual abuse and neglect of helpless children, and their separation from powerless families and communities.

The legacy of Indian residential schools has contributed to social problems that continue to exist in many communities today.

It has taken extraordinary courage for the thousands of survivors who have come forward to speak publicly about the abuse they suffered. It is a testament to their resilience as individuals and of the strengths of their cultures.

Regrettably, many former students are not with us today and died never having received a full apology from the Government of Canada.

The government recognizes that the absence of an apology has been an impediment to healing and reconciliation. Therefore on behalf of the Government of Canada and all Canadians, I stand before you, in this chamber so central to our life as a country, to apologize to Aboriginal peoples for Canada's role in the Indian residential school system.

To the approximately 80,000 living former students and all family members and communities, the Government of Canada now recognizes that it was wrong to forcibly remove children from their homes and we apologize for having done this.

We now recognize that in separating children from their families, we undermined the ability of many to adequately parent their own children and sowed the seeds for generations to follow, and we apologize for having done this.

We now recognize that far too often these institutions gave rise to abuse or neglect and were inadequately controlled, and we apologize for failing to protect you.

Not only did you suffer these abuses as children, but as you become parents, you were powerless to protect your own children from suffering the same experience and for this we are sorry.

The burden of this experience has been on your shoulders for far too long. The burden is properly ours as a government and as a country. There is no place in Canada for the attitudes that inspired the Indian residential school system to ever again prevail.

You have worked on recovering from this experience for a long time, and in a very real sense we are now joining you on this journey. The Government of Canada sincerely apologizes and asks the forgiveness of the aboriginal peoples of this country for failing so profoundly.

We are sorry.

A significant part of the abuse that was taking place at these residential schools was minimized and only mentioned in this apology. That is the sexual abuse of boys by pedophiles. An all-boy residential school is a lovely place for a pedophile to work because it affords a large pool of boys to groom as victims under minimal oversight.

Pedophilia is a sexual orientation that today is still criminalized for two reasons: first for the legal age of consent, second simply for consent itself. The defence or excuse a pedophile, as well any other sexual predator, often gives for his or her behaviour is that the age of consent is completely arbitrary and, therefore, unfair and unjust; it should be flexible. Then there is consent itself. Pedophiles do not just grab victims; they groom children to become victims. They create consent.

This is what Jeffry Epstein appears to believe, quite evident from the long history of his behaviour and conduct before his suspicious death in a New York City jail (although ruled a suicide, there are some who suspect it was murder). This is also what Harvey Weinstein believes. The Hollywood film producer was convicted of sex crimes in 2020. He believes he did nothing wrong. Sexual predators all feel like they are the victims of an unjust law. However, I say they have a mental health problem and an out-of-control addiction for which they need to take responsibility and accept the consequences. A lawyer from the Harvey Weinstein trial, said after the trial, "He got drunk on power and young struggling dreamers were not real people to him." What were they then? Are they then the creations of an alternate reality?

Now one more apology; On November 24, 2017, on behalf of the government of Canada, the Right Honorable Justin Trudeau, prime minister of Canada, delivered a tearful apology in the community of Goose Bay to former students and their families who attended the five residential schools that had been established and operating in Newfoundland and Labrador with the last school closing in 1980. This apology came a year after a class action lawsuit on behalf of the Indigenous people. The Liberal government agreed to distribute $50 million to the survivors who were left out of the original apology and settlement in 2008 from the Stephan Harper government.

Why these communities were not included in the previous apology by Prime Minister Harper and the monetary settlement at that time is unclear. Logically I would think it was because these schools were set up by the government of Newfoundland and Labrador before they joined the Confederation of Canada, so they were not run by the federal government. It is Newfoundland that should be apologizing and paying a settlement. I do not know if it has, but it looks like the blame shifted to the federal government for their involvement since Newfoundland joined confederation.

I would like to give you the full transcript of the apology as I think it is important that we know what was said on our behalf to our fellow Canadians. When we say something, we are accountable for it. But this goes far deeper than just words; it's about foundational values. This apology involves all Canadians.

The transcript can be found on Macleans.ca in an article by Catherine McIntyre November 24 2017 also the complete ceremony on YouTube by CBC NL Newfoundland and Labrador "Full apology Ceremony for Labrador resident School Survivors". (Last viewed 19-01-2021)

By way of introduction, I will point out a few things about Trudeau's apology. You notice Justin Trudeau speaks more in platitudes and lacks specifics and substance, quite unlike Stephen Harper's apology. Trudeau blames colonialism for the entire problem and the abuse. Does he really apologize, and is this how we apologize? As he states in his apology speech,

> "This is a shameful part of Canada's history—stemming from a legacy of colonialism. ... We must recognize the colonial way of thinking that fueled these practices. ... Cultures and traditions had been eroded by colonialism. It was in this climate that some experienced individual and family dysfunction, leaving a legacy that took many forms. ... Unfortunately, many of these intergenerational effects of colonialism on Indigenous people continue today".

He must assume we all know exactly what is meant by "colonial" and "colonialism." Surely it can't be the migration of people. And what is the colonial way of thinking that spans across three centuries? The residential schools were operating from 1870 to 1980. I would think the structure and curriculum of these schools would reflect that fact and be operated according to the best advice of the academia of that time. Then we need to consider what was popular thought and values in academia of that contemporary time. It was a time of declining popularity for the Utilitarian philosophy of John Stuart Mill and the coming rise of Evolutionism, Social Darwinism, Marxism, Nazism, and of Friedrich Nietzsche and Sigmund Freud. All these libertarian philosophies, ideologies, manifestos, and tyrannies stand in stark contrast to the biblical Covenant. It is little wonder, almost logical, that this time would be the triumphal age of anti-Semitism, the Holocaust, and pseudoscientific research on the evolution of humanity using indigenous people as research subjects. These residential schools were just a part of this and in the context of this contemporary mindset, a mindset that Justin Trudeau now dismisses as colonialism.

Now what is the mindset of Justin Trudeau and the Liberal government since he has just blamed the colonial way of thinking and dismissed it as wrong? Do they now embrace the biblical Covenant? Do they embrace the preamble to our Canadian Bill of Rights: "Founded on certain principles of the Supremacy of God and the Rule of Law"? Do they now recognize it as our defence against the encroachment of ideological tyranny, not just for Indigenous people, but for all Canadians, as is so well illustrated in Trudeau's apology to Indigenous people? How can anyone apologize for anything without being objective about reality? Or is this just another social contract apology of convenience?

I would like to reprint Justin Trudeau's entire speech for you, since it is short enough to be included in this book, and I find it good and worthwhile, as he states in his speech that "it should not be easily forgotten". I was hoping to get permission through the speaker of the House of Commons to republish this speech at the same time I asked for the permission for Stephan Harpers speech. However Justin Trudeau's apology was not give in Parliament and therefore not part of Parliamentary Hansard. I was directed to the Prime Minister website for permission since he has a copyright on it. I have sent him an email, but thus far there is no reply. Instead of asking again,(and I'm not going to keep waiting and even if I get permission) I will only highlight some of the speech that I find critical and therewith rely on fair use for research and analysis.

I think I will be well within my limits of fair use since the Supreme Court of Canada has stated that a large and liberal interpretation must be applied to all fair dealing purposes and not just for research. In a court judgment concerning CCH Canadian LTD v. Law Society of Upper Canada the Supreme Court of Canada established that "research, must be given a large and liberal interpretation in order to ensure that user rights are not unduly constrained ". On this basis I will give you some of the key ideas of His apology speech. It would not be much of an apology when we cannot have the benefit of its use because of copyright limitations.

His first, emphasis in his speech is on colonialism, the colonial way of thinking. As he states "We must recognize the colonial way of thinking that fueled these practices"; then in another place "stemming from a legacy of colonialism".

The next emphases is on the abuse these children suffered, they are listed as neglected, not properly clothed, and housed, physical and sexual abuse. They were deprived of the love and care of their parents, family and community. "Indigenous people were treated with a profound lack of equality and respect".

The third emphasis is on the damage to the family and community. Colonialism had eroded culture and traditions. "It was in this climate that some experienced individual and family dysfunction, leaving a legacy that took many forms. Afterwards, some experienced grief, poverty, family violence, substance abuse, family and community breakdown, and mental and physical health issues". Then he goes on to say, "Unfortunately, many of these intergenerational effects of colonialism on Indigenous people continue today". Then he blames colonialism again for regarding the indigenous ways of life as inferior and irrelevant.

The fourth emphasis in his conclusion he states "All Canadians possess the ability to learn from the past and shape the future". Then the last closing paragraph, "While we cannot forget the history that created these residential schools, we must not allow it to define the future. We call on all Canadians to take part in the next chapter – a time when Indigenous and non-Indigenous people build the future we want together".

Yes, Justin Trudeau, I agree with the last paragraph of your apology. But the future we want, that you think we should build together, can only be in the context of reality or you will be repeating the mistakes of the past. You have dismissed all our past wants as colonialism as if it were all some oppressive alternate reality, "a way of thinking." Should not our future wants and working together be rooted in objective reality and not based on the multitude of fantasies that the human mind is capable of? The only way of thinking that is sustainable is that which is rooted in reality. This is something everyone should be capable of recognizing. We can only refuse to our peril and demise.

On March 4, 2020, I read an article by Graham Dunbar of the Associated Press concerning the 2020 Summer Olympics scheduled for Tokyo, Japan. It concerned transgender athletes. The writer reports that "The IOC (International Olympic Committee) has decided it will wait until after the Tokyo Olympics to publish new guidelines on transgender athletes that are meant to protect inclusivity, safety, and fairness in sports."

One reason given for the decision was it is so few out of 11,000 athletes that it's much better to get it right than rushing out something just before the games. The discussion is about trying to get a balance between the views of transgender athletes and those who argue it is unfair to allow women who transitioned to compete with the physical advantage from being born male.

The writer went on to say that whatever is put in place will undoubtedly upset a lot of people. He said the talks had been, "a very difficult process, a very sensitive process, and there's no easy answer."

Now why did they not make a decision? Because they knew that transgender men who are now women are unfair competition in woman's competitive sports, but so far it's only 3 athletes out of the 11,000. Hopefully there will be no more, and the issue may be ignored or just go away.

However, it won't go away for these woman athletes who will be competing against these transgender people. Sports are activities of the mind and body, not just mind or what we might think or feel; to allow men who transgender to women to compete in women's sports is to destroy women's sports completely. What we are left with are men's sports and the other. It is anti-woman, an absurd cancel culture, canceling people and also real sports. They should compete in their own category since identity ideology is all about categories.

What I would say to the International Olympic Committee is this: Be aware that all ideological cultural manifestations of alternate realities eventually destroy themselves. Begin with the French Revolution and its revolutionary culture, then Soviet Marxist culture, German Nazi culture, and today's Western feminist culture, feminization, Pagan Marxist culture, and all the rest. In the words of the British historian David Starkey, "They go up themselves, (the Ideology) and destroy themselves. They are all full of themselves." In our time, with personalized internet media feeds, that process is greatly accelerated. Reality exists for a purpose that at some point in time, our absurd fantasies might get a reality check. We should pay attention to history.

When you say the talks have been, "a very difficult process, a very sensitive process and there are no easy answers," it is because you are watching this process of self-destruction. You need to say no to this. You need to return to reality because the people of the world will, despite ideological academia. All you can do when you side with this ideological academia is make people suffer. And in this case, it is real women and real sports. The world deserves much better.

Why is the new generation of young people in Western cultures sometimes called "snowflakes"? What makes them snowflakes? Why is there such identity confusion, experimental identities that cannot stand up to reality, are always in flux and changing, that melt at the least amount of criticism?

Babies are born with a biological sex, but apparently now in our time, without a gender identity. They can now choose gender identity independent of biology, so in the interim, they are to grow up gender-neutral. The possibilities are endless once you feel you are free from biology and reality.

You don't need to pick any gender at all, or you can be whatever you want to be whenever you want to be, and back again. You can be nonbinary or gender-fluid; you can choose whatever pronouns you like. Some examples of the growing list are they/theirs, theyby, ze, zim, and zer. I cannot keep up with it. And what if I get it wrong? But then what is there that yet could be wrong? Nevertheless, whatever they feel becomes automatically true, and you can't say a thing against it. When you do, you might even end up in jail. Yes, this is the twenty-first century. It is astonishing, at least for those of us who know some of the world's history and can make some logical comparisons.

Shall we now teach our children they are gender-neutral? Do we now give our children transgender toys and transgender teaching tools? Do we give them transgender media and movies to watch? Do we teach our children that they have all kinds of gender options and combinations of genders? Do we take our children to a gender specialist (a medical science specialist?) to explore the process of transitioning genders in a medical way? Do we give our children hormone therapy to suppress puberty when we think sex transition might be the best way forward?

All of this is happening in Canada, the United States, and most other Western countries. Is this not child abuse? Is this not grooming children to construct consent for abuse by alternate reality? Or is this our transition from evolutionism to intelligent design?

Children are procured from a biological mother and father. Do children then choose same-sex parents? Where are the human rights for children? Are they no longer human beings?

All of this is led by the Western academia of ideological Social Pagan Marxism, a revolutionary deconstructionism to destroy all human rights and make people into the creations of an alternate reality for the purpose of their tyranny because they are going to save the world.

This is the same colonialism or colonial way of thinking that Justin Trudeau dismissed as wrong and apologized for just a few years ago. He is very right in expressing the damage it does and the suffering it causes children, families, and communities. He is also very right in supporting the class action lawsuit and subsequent monetary settlement for the abuse these children, families, and communities have suffered.

Is all of Canada—and you may as well also say most of the world—now a residential school to re-educate the population to conform to the ideological correctness defined by the Western academia of Social Pagan Marxism? All the evidence I see indicates it is.

Stephen Harper mentions in his and Canada's apology to Indigenous Canadians that it was at times said the purpose behind the policy of these residential schools was to kill the Indian in the Indian. By comparison I see this modern Western ideological academia has the intention to kill the Christian in the Christian, to kill the Jew in the Jew. But it goes deeper than this. It's about killing the human being in the human. It is the human instinct for justice they want to kill by bringing it into confusion.

This instinct is part of being created in the image of God. The ideologist calls it evolving to be your own god. (They may be oblivious to it, but it is the evidence). There is a profound difference with serious consequences for responsibility, accountability, human rights, human cooperation, and stewardship. It is the difference between humility and arrogance toward God's creation and its reality. But then how could you have any value toward evolving? They live on a different planet, different galaxy one that in time will not be big enough for one person.

All those young people, those now called snowflakes and the generations from the last fifty years, are victims of ideological indoctrination. I think your victimization is much worse than you realize. You have been destabilized. You need to educate yourself about it. You need to sue the government and academia for having been lied to. You have been taught ideology, not knowledge.

The little knowledge you may have been taught is often wrapped in ideology completely irrelevant to the subject. Conrad Black in his book "The Canadian Manifesto" (A book you should read) writes "The State schools in almost every advanced western society have been virtually destroyed....this is one of the most implacable symptoms of a decaying society; the collapse into illiterate and arrogant know-nothingism of the State school system. The most improbable and threadbare disciplines are being stretched into university subjects."

In his apology to Indigenous Canadians, Justin Trudeau clearly described the damage caused by ideological tyranny in our schools and government administration. I am sure he would hold such values for all Canadians and that he does understand the injustice of a double standard. I will give you a few examples from his apology speech, with my substitute of Ideology for Colonialism, to unmask the deception and misplaced blame.

> "We must recognize the colonial (Ideological) way of thinking that fueled these practices".

> "Children who returned from traumatic experiences in these schools looked to their families and communities for support but, in many cases found that their own practices, cultures and traditions had been eroded by colonialism (ideology). It was in this climate that some experienced individual and family dysfunction, leaving a legacy that took many forms. Afterwards, some experienced grief,

poverty, family violence, substance abuse, family and community breakdown, and mental and physical health issues. Unfortunately, many of these intergenerational effects of colonialism (ideology) on Indigenous people continue today......

....We are sorry for the misguided belief that Indigenous children could only be properly provided for, cared for, or educated if they were separated from the influence of their families, traditions and cultures. This is a shameful part of Canada's history—stemming from a legacy of colonialism (ideology), when Indigenous people were treated with a profound lack of equality and respect—a time in our country when we undervalued Indigenous cultures and traditions and it was wrongly believed Indigenous languages, spiritual beliefs and ways of life were inferior and irrelevant".

Is all of this within the context of the covenant relationship, the supremacy of God and the rule of law that includes everyone, and should have always included Indigenous Canadians? Or is it just borrowed from the biblical Covenant for the present purpose by another ideology from another alternate reality that does not think itself as colonialism? Or are they just ignorant of their own biases from an ideology that clearly believes objective reality is inferior and irrelevant?

How do we go about getting justice?

First, we need judges in the courts who are not of any ideological alternate reality. We need judges in the courts who will defend the constitution, real and objective human rights, judges who understand the meaning of our preamble to the Canadian Bill of Rights, "founded on certain principles of the Supremacy of God and the Rule of Law." This is the requirement to be objective concerning creation and reality. This is also our defence against tyranny. Only then is there any chance of winning anything against this ideology in our courts. We need to elect a government that is not ideological but covenantal and will appoint judges who, in turn, will defend our constitution and real human rights.

Second, everyone needs to complain about the ideology and refuse ideology in our schools and universities. To be effective in this regard you need to get your education from outside of the mainstream. Search out historic and conservative sources for justice, human rights, constitutional rights, objective truth, and objective reality. There is a reason mainstream academia would like to ban or block conservatives from universities and the internet. You might learn some truth, which is a threat to them and to all ideologies. You need to learn real truth supported by facts and use it. We need to defeat the systemic ideological elitism in our universities.

Conservative means to conserve and protect from harm: today that means the constitution our human rights and freedom found in a covenantal relationship with truth and reality. It is not turning the clock back in time like Ideology would like to teach, that is in fact what ideology would like to do, turn back to pagan ideology.

Now for the third apology. President Francois Mitterrand of France in 1985 announced a formal apology to all the descendants of the French Huguenots to mark the tri-centenary of the revocation of the Edict of Nantes. You will probably wonder what all of this is about. If you have been taught ideology for history, you won't know. And if you have been taught some good history, you still might not know. If you are a descendant of French Huguenots, you might not know. It is a part of history that ideology prefers to ignore.

Our family, as well as many Dutch-Canadian families, are also descendants of French Huguenot refugees. I will give you some of the history. In 1685, in France, King Louis XIV, known as the "Sun King," intended to make France 100 per cent Roman Catholic again by making it against the law to be Protestant Christian. You had to convert back to the Roman Catholic religion.

This conversion was enforced by the law. It became war on the Protestants. It was persecution, prison, slavery, and death for Protestant Christians. Many fled as refugees to countries in all parts of the world where they could be free. Untold hundreds of thousands of people were displaced. These French Huguenots where not just poor French peasants; they spanned the entire social structure of France, from nobility to peasant. Many of them were artisans, contractors, businesspeople, and intellectuals. This growing Protestant faith, which was covenantal in religious practice and life, was perceived as a threat to the absolutism of the French monarchy, the pope, and the Roman Catholic church. Because covenantal values give rise to constitutional government and human rights, something that is very unsettling to the aspirations of ideological tyranny, the Protestants had to go.

The Edict of Nantes that was revoked had been in force for eighty-seven years. The edict was issued in 1598 by King Henry IV, a Roman Catholic with close ties to Protestants. The edict granted freedom of conscience to Protestants and freedom of religion in their own churches. The Edict of Nantes was to put an end to the French religious civil war between Roman Catholics and Protestants. Ever since the beginning of the Protestant Reformation and the French reformer, John Calvin, there was persecution of the Protestants in France led by Roman Catholic nobles. As the number of Protestants increased, the persecution escalated into civil war.

The Edict of Nantes brought peace for a short time. But it was soon ignored, and the persecution of the Protestants resumed. The most the edict may have accomplished was the prevention full-scale civil war until it was revoked in 1685 by King Louis XIV.

With the loss of the Protestants through the revocation of the Edict of Nantes, France also lost much of its economic capacity and wealth. But it did gain security for the despotism of the king, the pope, the Roman Catholic church, and nobles. That was until the French Revolution.

In 1789, 103 years after the revocation of the Edict of Nantes, this ideological despotism of the French monarchy and the Roman Catholic church's clericalism all came to an end. They lost their heads to a device of their own invention, the guillotine, in the French Revolution. They were replaced this time not by the biblical Covenant and the concepts of constitutional government of the Protestant Reformation but by its imitation, the social contract, another ideological alternate reality that can be as cruel as themselves. It was the beginning of political correctness as a culture, a dangerous culture that had the guillotine as backup. This revolutionary culture was constantly in flux and eventually produced Napoleon, his wars, his military defeats, and his final famous defeat at the Battle of Waterloo. The latter was a reality check for France and an end to the revolutionary culture of political correctness; at least for the time.

What do I think about President Francois Mitterrand's apology to French Huguenots, now three hundred years later? First, I was not aware there was such an apology back in 1985. Trying to research it, I can't seem to find a copy of the apology in English. I have found a French copy, but my French is not so good. I contacted several Huguenot societies around the world and asked if they had a copy in English, but none did. The Huguenot museum in Germany could come up with nothing. I sent a request to France's Ministry of Information; they replied that there was none available. They must think that we descendants of the French Huguenots in the Diaspora are still speaking French. Or are they just speaking to themselves?

What I did find on my internet search was an article from the *Los Angeles Times* on the apology. It focused on the ignorance of people concerning this history. According to the article, the French Post Office issued a commemorative stamp that mixed up the history completely. The stamp's legend proclaimed, "1685–1985 Welcome of the Huguenots, Tolerance, Plurality, and Fraternity."

The persecution began in earnest again in 1685 and was in force until the French Revolution, more than one hundred years later. Is this a welcoming tolerance, plurality, and fraternity? No thanks. You have got your history wrong.

There is not much left of French culture among the Huguenots in the Diaspora. After more than two hundred years of official and unofficial persecution, there is not much incentive to be French. The betrayals have taken their toll; we assimilated with other like-minded Protestants around the world.

An apology is for something that has become recognized as a wrong and unjust. Then, it is also reasonable to speculate what things could have been like if the practice, the incident had not occurred. If the French monarchy and government would have stayed its course and enforced the Edict of Nantes, the state of France would eventually have become a constitutional monarchy with human rights. It would have become a prosperous state under the supremacy of God and the rule of law founded on the biblical Covenant. This would have happened based on the public will of the French Protestants. As a result, the French Revolution would not have happened, and then neither Napoleon nor the war. History would have been much different. The only constant thing that can be learned from this history is that either way, it was the tyranny from the Roman Catholic church and the French monarchy that had to go; it was too much for the people. Alternate realities that do not add up in logic and in justice, and ignore the fact people have rational minds, will always lead to division and war.

Francois Mitterrand was France's first Socialist president. While this indicates his values and those of the government, on what is the apology based? Is it a secular apology of tolerance? The things we say and do are never baseless. Would secular now be based on objective reality, the Covenant? - On real freedom, not just tolerance?

Freedom of religion and religious tolerance can never be the freedom to persecute and engage in human sacrifice; that is a contradiction. You cannot use religion to destroy religion or the religious. Religion is required to be objective in order to be free. Likewise, self-defence is a human right that begins with freedom of speech. You cannot use human rights to disarm your neighbour from his or her self-defence. That is also a contradiction. To have freedom of religion requires religion and its institutions to be objective. To have human rights requires justice and government to be objective. To sustain both requires a people who are covenantal.

In summary and as advice from a descendent of the French Huguenots, I would say this. Before the Protestant Reformation, about five hundred years ago and earlier, ideology was dressed up as Christian religion having authority over knowledge, requiring you to conform to it, its dictates and control. Civility and grace were dispensed as rewards for obedience. Jesus Christ and salvation were prerequisites dispensed as merchandise. And only then was there any common grace. You were not allowed to have or read the Bible. For the common people to have any real knowledge was dangerous.

In contrast, for the French Huguenots and all the Protestant Reformation, the Bible, its grace, and knowledge were for all people, and in the Bible we find salvation in Jesus Christ. Grace is a gift from God. None of this is dependent on an ideological authority. It is the moral law and God's justice that gives us our civil freedom and the context for the gospel of salvation in Jesus Christ, as well as all knowledge. We live under the Covenant of grace and its moral rule of law, where everyone should share in knowledge and are not subject to ideological tyranny for an official interpretation and its use in order to alter reality and enforce an ideological faith. Simply said we recognize justice and reject Ideology. It is for all of this we were severely persecuted for more than two hundred years.

After this came the French Revolution. Between the Reformation that was refused and today came the social contract of this Revolution, the beginning of secularism and political correctness—with the backup of the guillotine, a human correctness that denies sin and repentance, putting into motion for the world two hundred years of ideological revolutions of one ideology up against another, genocide, ethnic cleansing, and the Holocaust.

Today ideology is dressed up as secularism, again a religion of elitism believing to have authority and governance over knowledge, leveraging away our human rights and the common grace; An ideology constantly searching for new opportunities and constructing alternate realities, anything that might mislead people, make them fearful, and to look to the elite for everything, to give up their rights for a greater good, the elite. What God has given us free they will make into merchandise to be dispensed on obedience as privilege or reward. When ideology controls knowledge, knowledge is destroyed. Then the Covenant and common grace are destroyed. What they want is the utopian state that I mentioned at the beginning of this book, the Mayan, a state of total control by the priests and where cruelty and sacrifice were the ultimate in piety. When ideology is in control of science and knowledge, we are in serious trouble, and danger.

We live in a world where mostly the blind leads the blind from ideology to ideology. That is the problem we need to solve; the Covenant is offered for the solution. That reaches all the way back in religious history to the ban on human sacrifice because God will provide.

Having said that, you might understand why we were so persecuted in the past and are still hated by many, especially ideologists. You might also have a better understanding of anti-Semitism and how it relates to this Covenant. You might understand why we must have academic freedom and freedom of speech. It's in debate that we discover truth. We do not shut down debate to protect ideology from truth and defeat.

This might help you understand why so many Huguenots and other Protestants were so active in helping Jews escape Nazi authorities in the last World War.

This might also explain to you why we are pro-life. We are for stewardship, responsibility, and accountability, but also for repentance and forgiveness. In objective life we live the Covenant, believing in God; in subjective faith, we believe in Jesus Christ, our Saviour from sin, and our righteousness. And in turn, confirming objective life in creation and reality for all is of God to His glory, and forever.

Going back to Mitterrand's apology speech, since the French government did not provide an official English translation and I can't find any others, I will rely on Google translate for an English translation and share it here with you. The quality and accuracy of the translation have not been verified, and I can give no opinion on it, but I will use it here as a guide to the French.

First, a few introductory comments. Mitterrand, in his speech, defends the Reformation as the struggle not being for tolerance but for freedom. I agree. I have always understood that it is truth that makes us free. Then further in his speech he refers to a common good without defining what that is. However, the whole speech and apology are about that common good.

Then in the context for his speech, I would think the common good would be the objective interpretation of God's creation and reality. Or as taken from his speech, "Defend what is common and make the essential prevail". In opposition to this, how could a subjective interpretation of God's creation and reality, in the ever-evolving pragmatism of ideology—denying us our freedom of conscience, freedom of speech, and academic freedom—ever be considered as the common good? Again from his speech, "But that State crosses these limits, that wants to govern the conscience and hearts. It forgets where its true role is, more simply, he renounces, and helplessly witnesses the unleashing of passions and there is no longer, in the end and for no one, either order or freedom,"

You need to read his speech carefully. You might recognize that Western Marxist liberalism, paganism of today is far on the way to eliminating our freedoms by the deconstruction of constitutional human rights and reconstructing ideological interpretations that are enforced as a mandatory ideological state religion that will have consequences no different than all the world's tragedies of the past, of which the dismantling and eventual revocation of the Edict of Nantes was one.

You cannot have state religion and freedom of conscience. Nor can you have an ideological state and freedom of conscience as they are the same things. Faith and religion itself are not the problem, but religion, like politics, when they become ideological, they are the problem. They then are the same tyranny, opposing the Covenantal, (the truth that makes us free).

Today in Western states we are witnessing the revocation of constitutional governments and human rights with all our freedoms. We need to stop this. We will have freedom.

It is becoming very clear that abortion, infanticide, eugenics, ethnic cleansing, and genocide are all elements of Western elitist ideological governments, and the targets for their ethnic cleansing are Christians and Jews and the Covenant. In order for ideology to be successful, ethnic cleansing is essential. Think about it as you read Mitterrand's speech, and decide for yourself.

The Address by Mr. Francois Mitterrand, President of the Republic, at the Revocation of the Edict of Nantes, on tolerance in political and religious matters and the history of Protestantism in France, Paris UNESCO Palace, Friday October 11 1985.

Full Text from *Vie-Pubique Au Coeur du debat public.*

Ladies and Gentlemen,

Three hundred years ago—we said it and this is the reason for your presence—King Louis XIV revoked the Edict of Nantes, signed by Henri IV, his ancestor. An act of government for contemporaries, one act among many others, no more, no less significant, no doubt, than other decisions taken during this long reign.

How does this memory bring us together today? How is it that this date speaks to us with so much demand, to the point of justifying a commemoration?

The Revocation as an event, the historical fact itself could seem foreign to us, distant. The prohibition on Protestants to practice their religion in France, it would suffice to say that it belongs to a bygone era. What good is it, after all, to use the beautiful expression of Marc Bloch, speaking of his profession as a historian "out of macabre dilection, to untie the dead gods". This is because the Revocation is one of those great moments when fate changes.

The persecution of a minority who has become, with the stroke of the pen, outlaws in their own country. This brings us back to realities close to us. This gangrene still lasts. We know the horror of it; humanity is never cured of it. Commemorating the Revocation is therefore a serious gesture. Others than me will put the past in the dock, at the risk of taking a moralistic look, full of anachronisms on 17th century society.

But the Revocation is first of all its reverse, its opposite, this Edict of Nantes promulgated in 1598, to put an end to 30 years of civil war and to extinguish a tirelessly revived inferno, which after having devastated France, threatened its very existence, as a state. Finding the means of coexistence between the Catholic majority and the Huguenot minority was first of all to exclude the prospect of one over the other, it was to refuse the solution that each had adopted for its own sake. Share, Spain and England, the unity of religion imposed by the Terror, this meant forcing the warring factions to accept another logic that was superior to them. The reason of the state, depositary and guarantor of the national interest, that in France, since the High Middle Ages we call: the common good.

It was up to the state to make triumph what was not of the order of religion, faith, individual conscience, where the state has nothing to do. But of the order of politics, since what was in danger was the nation, And this third party, whose efforts lead, after so many failed attempts, to the Edict of Nantes, it had been given, remember, this beautiful name—allow me to be sensitive to it—"the politicians"; some belonging to the Reformation, others being faithful to Rome. They too could have fought eternally to avenge Coligny or the Duke of Guise. But coming from both religions, they first thought of France, of exhausted torn France, which could no longer take it. Supporting each other, to France, whose very life was at stake. The Edict of Nantes is the work of that; it is so true that throughout history, it is only around France that we have been able to gather the French! Thus in these particularities, as in the inadequacies that the modern mind, accustomed to religious freedom, can find in it, the Edict of Nantes includes a teaching; it establishes in a way specific to the period in question, a precarious, difficult but real balance between the social weight of the majority, the specific rights of a minority and the common interest embodied by the state. The Edit is a compromise, in the best sense of the term. A compromise of which the political power vouches.

He asks each community, without renouncing its convictions, to accept a limit; the place of the other.

Catholics dreamed of re-establishing a single religion in France: policies make it clear to them that they have the right to use only spiritual weapons to achieve this right. Internal reform, the renewal of spiritual weapons to achieve this right. Internal reform, the renewal of spirituality, controversy, mission ... The Protestants had constituted a military, political and religious force to believe, to pray in their own way. But the State, while giving them guarantees, imposed certain constraints on them. To preserve the political unity of the Nation, there will be no State within the State. In short, the Edict of Nantes, after all these heartbreaks, reminds us that everyone is first and foremost French. And it would certainly be an anachronism to read in advance in the Edict of Nantes the declaration of Human Rights—you said it. Mr President—or the secularism of the State. But, when we consider the history of France, in a long-term perspective, we can perceive as a stage—and an important stage—in the gradual and slow conquest of these two foundations of our Republic.

Exceptionally, in Europe at the time, from 1598, members of a religious minority could profess their belief—that of the Reformation religion—without incurring penalties in their career and even, more simply, in their everyday life.

Even more astonishing measure—in the spirit of the times—it becomes possible, without ceasing to be French recognized as such, to change religion. It is no longer simply a question of transforming an open conflict into coexistence, on the basis of a status quo, but of the birth certificate of freedom of conscience, the origin of all freedom. In the very hierarchical society of the time, where illiteracy was the lot of the greatest number, the political power dared to establish the right of the fragile, of the obscure individual conscience. He dared to hand over to each one this capital decision: the choice of his faith, of his religion. While such a decision depended—it was believed—on eternal salvation or the pains of hell that would never end.

Sixty years later, sixty year later began again the time of turmoil. For a quarter of a century, the Edict of Nantes was to be gradually dismantled, before being revoked. To do justice to historical truth, we must not confuse the brutal persecution which eventually prevailed with the desire to re-establish the religious unity of the kingdom, which was believed to be possible by less violent means. But it is precisely this inexorable spiral that will end in galleys, gibbets, and pyres.

The failure of each measure led to take a new one—we know the process—harsher, which was juxtaposed with the previous one, without necessarily abolishing it. There was the legal cold war which began with the interpretation of the Edict in a pinch. They argued over the letter; we ended up fabricating, to measure, new laws that went against specific articles of the Edict. There was the conversion fund. Based on the idea that the lure of profit chased away what were called "bad feelings". And that corruption made it possible to avoid violence.

And then, faced with his failure, we came to the kidnappings of children, the dragonnades—it's a story that you know—blind terror, moral torture, where a word, a only one word—I abjure—for the nightmare to end.

By proclaiming freedom of conscience without abolishing the state religion, the Edict of Nantes had half opened a door, but far from growing, the opening closed like a tomb.

Double lesson: faced with violence, fanaticism, the chain of aggressions and reprisals, it is the State which restores peace; it is the primacy of the political which founds, by limiting the ambitions of freedoms, religions, and first of all conscience, But by that very fact, he accepts to set limits for himself, not to exceed the limit which he has imposed on himself. It stops where the irreducible freedom of every human being begins, a freedom that would not exist if it were not there to protect and guarantee it. And all this while being faithful; faithful to its mission which is to jealously watch over the interests of the motherland, But that the State crosses these limits that it wants to govern the conscience and the hearts, it forgets where its true role is, more simply, he renounces and helplessly witnesses the unleashing of passions and there is no longer, in the end and for no one, either order or freedom.

The Edict of Nantes, it should be known, was very unpopular and basically, it did not satisfy anyone. While the Revocation, it was enthusiastically approved by a very large majority. And only outside the Protestant community—it goes without saying a few isolated voices opposed it. Discerning the long-term interest of a country, without letting itself be diverted from its duty, its principles, its objectives, by the ups and downs of public opinion, this is not the easiest path. But it is the one where there are the fewest mistakes. At the time of the Revocation, power counted on the loyalty of the Huguenots—Mademoiselle du Corbier made it very clear—and as Mazarin had declared "the little herd grazes on weeds but does not move away". He had not listened attentively to certain warnings like that of the two pastors of Languedoc claiming to have—I quote them—"with the intention of carrying their obedience to the orders of His Majasty as far as their conscience allowed them". He thought that it would be enough to add to the violence of the dragons this decisive word; "the King wants it" only then, the first moment of stupor passed, loyalty changed its name: it became resistance.

Despite a formal ban—think about it" on very unusual surveillance at the time 250,000 French Protestants left for countries of refuge. I tell you, it is not without emotion that even 300 years later, the President of the French Republic evokes this emigration and the presence here of descendants of these Huguenots adds to my sorrow. Better than anyone else Michelet was able to capture the intensity of such an exile. He wrote; "Emigration was very difficult, its greatest obstacle was in the very souls of those who had to take this step. It seemed too strong to uproot themselves from here, to break with so many living fibers, to leave friends and relatives, all their old habits, their childhood home, their family home, the cemeteries where theirs lay. This cruel France, however, cannot be parted with without great effort and without mortal regret".

For members of the industrious bourgeoisie, craftsmen and creators of new techniques—you recalled it—mademoiselle, Mr, President, but that we did not know much in the 19th century— the peasant elite—you must have traveled the Cevennes or my native Charentes to find out— the refugees donated their qualities to their host countries. And since at this rostrum, a Dutch Huguenot symbolizes the exodus undergone and the hospitality received, let us remember that the fugitives brought and developed in the Netherlands many techniques which had their value and which justified your remark on the fact that we received them wholeheartedly, but also to the fact that we relied a little on them to launch the tired economy of the moment: headgear, silk, sheets with which militias were so often dressed, serges, crepons, gold and silver embroidery. But above all, you recalled it for the printing press and the bookshops; freedom of opinion flourished in this country already more tolerant than most of the Nations of Europe and many because of it.

We saw their developing a kind of ecumenism already that of mutual aid; the Catholics and Dutch Jews participating in the collections carried out in favor of the exiles. And we must add, for the honor of our country, that in Germany, on the registers of the crossroads city of Frankfurt am Main, the hub of the journey to the refuge, we find, yes we find the trace, not only of many Huguenots, of course, but also French Catholics banished from the kingdom for having helped Protestants. All solidarity has therefore not been absent from our people at this decisive moment.

It is in Les Miserables that Victor Hugo stages a "poor Huguenot woman—it is he who speaks—under Louis-le-Grand, who sees her newborn being taken just before breastfeeding her and the executioner said to the woman, mother and nurse: "Abjure" give her to choose between the death of her child and the death of her conscience". I would like to note in this regard that the resistance of this woman commands admiration; that of these mothers— who transmitted every night, the forbidden Protestant education. That of the prisoners of the Tower of Constance—you mentioned this very beautiful film which recalled this tragic story—in this fortress where they prayed, where they sang psalms, where they celebrated worship, showing in the most exemplary way the paradoxical situation experienced by prisoners of conscience deprived of their liberty: to be free at last, precisely because in prison, to acquire freedom of the mind. Precisely at the cost of sacrifice and freedom of the body! What I am saying there; who is it or which one of you.

Whatever its confession of the religion of which it claims. Which did not live it or which did not know by its ancestors, or which does not know it by those of his confession, which is worthy in other countries where persecution exists, who thus escaped this misery, this protest, this affirmation, and finally this victorious courage? But at what cost ... suffering, blood, death, sometimes forgetting to be free at last, precisely because in prison, to acquire freedom of the mind, precisely at the cost of sacrifice and the freedom of the body. But at what cost ...

Historians today have designated the romantic apology for the Reformation, the mother of the Revolution. I believe they are right. 1798 belongs to the whole of the French people. But it is not indifferent that the elements which structured French Protestantism, from the 16th and 17th centuries, contributed to make it unbearable to the supporters of absolutism. I will name Robeau ST-Etienne, who himself was to be a victim of the Revolution after a life so laden with storms, exiles, proscriptions. He was a pastor. But he was able to pronounce from the tribune of the Constituent, during the elaboration of the declaration of the Rights of Man and of the Citizen, the formula which has remained famous, forgive me for quoting it but it is beautiful: "This is not even the tolerance that I claim; it is freedom" I myself have used the word tolerance several times today already. And those who preceded me did as I did. And yet that is what it is: is the real debate of the Revocation. We are mistaken when we believe that the choice is between tolerance and intolerance. Intolerance is a state on mind—always dangerous—tolerance is revoked. What had to be established and defended was freedom, but freedom implies as many duties as rights. It cannot mean withdrawal into oneself, the simple right for individuals to escape the constraints of life. In common freedom with us, or at least what I know. Is also the control of the State by all citizens, thanks to the mechanisms of democracy and I have endeavored to ensure that these mechanisms broaden their hold, so that the citizen can exist in front of the State, so that the State is the expression of the citizens ...

In the 19th century, Protestant vitality was one of the forces which made the democratic idea mature and made values triumph, the Revolution. It shows apparent paradox and deep coherence, a rediscovered fervor. And in the realm of politics, a resolute action that has been called the secularism of the State, a kind of dissociation of temporal and the spiritual, without denying either on or the other. Complementary for the life of each and however different in the management of the State, constituting the best guarantor of full religious freedom, on condition, of course, of not wanting this freedom only for oneself. "The honor of a religion is that one cannot practice it"—exclaimed the pastor of Pressence from the tribune of the Chamber during the moral order, and in contradiction with the moral order. And the same Pressence, at the solemn moment of the commemoration—the same—of the bicentenary of the Revocation, added that Protestantism would be ready, if necessary, to defend the freedom of Catholicism if ever anticlericalism were to undermine it. This language intersects this dialogue across time and across space,—those who are here, I can see it clearly, it is the language they want, undoubtedly feeling deeply that it is the same threats that, today are before them, establishing through ecumenical dialogue new relations with Catholicism, Protestantism, I think, has not forgotten, cannot forget its tormented history of minorities.

We remember the action of Pastor Boegner, particularly—there are many others of course, and of all faiths—against anti-Jewish laws during the Occupation, and that, more recent of the Cimade in favor of immigrant workers.

The Republic knows what can bring to the national community the reflection of the religious present in France on the problems of society. Ladies and gentlemen, if the Republic guarantees you freedom, your spiritual influence that is your business; no one can take care of it for you. Your contribution to the history of France—which will symbolize tomorrow; the performance of the first tragedy written in French and due to the reformer Theodore de Beze, who I have often met in my itineraries around Vezelay—it is up to you to continue to enrich by remaining one of the living thought families of this country.

The Republic guarantees everyone the freedom to believe or not to believe. It refuses to choose between the French because of their religion— which I repeat that it does not have to know—and if it does not include in its laws any worship, it is not by indifference, it is that its task is to unite the French by other means,—because religious search is also the search for unity—which are those of another order. Defend what is common, make the essential prevail.

What makes France, beyond particularisims, what it is? A presence in the world, a continuity in history; it haunts my mind every day. We have just mentioned many values in connection with Revocation; it is undoubtedly because we feel that these values remain current. The one who has not chosen the same route, the one who comes from elsewhere, must we therefore rule out, wanting France to be welcoming to those who have chosen to live there, and who at the same time—who will blame them—want to remain themselves. Knowing how to make everyone accept and even love, more and better than the particularities, the differences to which each one is attached; France as it is and the Republic which serves it. Old story, the dragonnades, the galleys, the camisards? No, today's story around the world. Vertigo of exclusion, rejection of minorities, temptation to push towards exile—and to what refuge—a part of those who live with us. It exists, it walks in some minds.

That is why, ladies and gentlemen, the memory of the Revocation must help us to prevail the spirit in which is commemorated this tercentenary—painful anniversary, one of the most painful among the painful in a long history of France—with the hope of seeing France together, for the most part, naturally.

There are common tasks; we won't refuse anyone. By always ensuring that freedom of conscience and equality of rights are preserved and in return only asking for a better practice of fraternity, a more constant search for the necessary equality.

This is why I will tell you in conclusion; let us find new reasons to believe in this freedom. In the memory of one persecution among others, but one of the bloodiest in our history of France, I repeat it again; we will be able to draw lessons of fidelity and courage. In the memory of divisions, tears or tears, one will find the strength to work for unity of the fatherland. Because there is a generation, mine, that of many others, here in this assembly, a generation which lived in its youth another drama of exclusion; the choice of death against conscience or death with his conscience; and what we lived, how could we forget it? There is only one duty left: that of teaching it to those who will follow us.

8

GLOBALISM AND THE COVENANT

I have read several books on globalism. I picked up on it as a subject because there was a progressive academia pushing globalism as some modern concept, at least there was before Trump. I wanted to know what they were hyped up about. I support fair trade but not free trade. I have known for a long time that international trade is not fair when we utilize tyranny and communism to provide cheap labour to replace Western labour, and then put us into debt to them through trade imbalances. I began to wonder if the word "wrong" had any meaning in the West. Today we are beginning to see how wrong and misguided they were. I have waited twenty years for a US president like Donald Trump.

For the purpose of this chapter, I begin with where we are today. As I sit and write this, we are at the beginning of the coronavirus-19 lockdown in order to slow and reduce the spread of the virus. This is the kind of globalism no one seems to consider. As a farmer and environmentalist, I have seen much of the devastation done to the native American ecology by bringing over and introducing exotic foreign pests, species, and diseases. This should not be done. We should be much more sensitive to local and regional ecologies and economies. Human pandemics can be expected to occur. We should always be prepared for them so that they can be stopped where they begin. This takes international co-operation.

I was scrolling through Google news feeds on my computer, just reading the headlines. All the headlines seemed to be quite positive except for one that had a negative connotation: "Donald Trump issues state of emergency after having down played corona virus." I am sure President Donald Trump has said some things that can be perceived as downplaying the threat of the virus; you surely do not want him exciting hysteria and panic either. If I remember correctly, was not President Donald Trump called racist a month ago for restricting travel to and from China and for calling the virus the Chinese virus? Apparently we should not identify a disease by the place of its origin; that is racist. At that time it was the media that was downplaying the threat of the virus. Then why do they not just write, "President Donald Trump issues a state of emergency after an increase in coronavirus infections"? Did I read this news story? No. I have read it before; it is predictable. I know what it is about. I shut it down and went to the real news. Attacking people is not news; it is the derangement of the media.

I remember watching a White House press conference three and half years ago. I think it was when Prime Minister Teresa May of Great Britain was on a state visit to the United States just after Donald Trump was sworn in as president. President Donald Trump was defending his economic policies of putting America first in trade and his intention to renegotiate American trade agreements and bring back the American supply chain and jobs to the United States; in other words, protectionism for the American worker and their economy. Reporters were asking questions about American isolationism. They were substituting isolationism for protectionism. Their intended narrative was that President Donald Trump was going to destroy the American economy by taking the country back into isolationism. This is the news they were trying to construct. Donald Trump pointed out to them that protectionism is not isolationism. And there you have your evidence for your fake news. If they still have not yet learned the difference, now with the corona virus, they might discover what isolationism really is.

What this unintended isolationism really illustrates is the need for local and regional economies to be self-reliant and not dependent on international trade. Every state needs to have a large degree of economic security. It is irresponsible that most of our medical supplies and medicines are made in China. This dependency on imports compromises national security, and all the shipping necessary to utilize cheap foreign labour does nothing to improve protection of the environment. Rather, this dependency on trade is hostile to the environment.

One more thing that can be learned from the present pandemic is the failure of alternate realities. The pandemic began in Wuhan, China, probably in November 2019. If the immediate response to this new virus, its discovery, and its outbreak had been honest and truthful and held in an open public discussion, the virus could have been prevented from becoming a global pandemic. The alternate reality of Chinese communism as any alternate reality always need to construct an ideologically correct response to everything. They survive on officially constructed truth—propaganda—and, therefore, cannot tolerate freedom of speech. Any immediate and spontaneous response coming from the people who know is not allowed. As a result, alternate realities are at first always a denial. Then by the time their official ideological correct response is made available, it is too late. It is this communist alternate reality that should be held responsible for the global pandemic.

If China wants to be a civilized trading partner, it needs to begin with objective human rights, freedom of speech, and academic freedom. However, to be effectual requires the biblical Covenant. That should not be a problem as China already has millions of Christians. The Chinese government needs to stop the persecution of its people.

Likewise, our ideological left alternate reality in the West survives on constructed talking points. When we confront them with the truth, they scream racism. It is the only response they can achieve after being derailed. The word "racism," along with a whole list of other words, is used by the ideological left to mean, "Shut up." It is not surprising that the American ideological left has become useful for Chinese propaganda. For us to protect our freedoms and take back our freedom of speech, we need to be upfront with the truth and the facts all the time and not back down.

The unfortunate tragedy with ideologists and their alternate reality is that they are always right and, therefore, unforgiving. The Covenant, in contrast, recognizes the imperfect human being and is forgiving. For that reason, we require freedom of speech. Through it we can achieve the best proximity to truth and justice and at times, the mark itself.

When I was in Israel, I became friends with a man about my own age. He and his wife had immigrated to Israel from Kazakhstan. After the collapse of the Soviet Union in 1991, many Russian Jews moved to Israel. This man was born and grew up in the Soviet Union. He was educated in the communist school system. He lived most of his life under the relentless persuasion of communist ideology and propaganda, yet none of this influenced him. He did not have those values; he could see through the ideology and recognize its falseness. He was a Messianic Jew, rooted and grounded in the Covenant. He was grounded on a firm foundation of objective reality, not on ideology, but on a faith that was illegal in the Soviet Union and could get you thrown in jail or labour camps. It could even mean one's death.

By comparison, I was born in the Netherlands and grew up in rural Ontario, Canada. I was educated in the public-school system, which was once designated to be the Protestant school system but over time became ideological schools. I also live in an environment with relentless propaganda and advertising that is political and commercial consumerism. It all comes from an ideological academia and Hollywood, and it is the same ideology I am writing about in this book. I have also become quite immune to it. I do not subscribe to any of it. It does not influence me because I can see the falseness, the contradictions, the hypocrisy, the arbitrariness. I am also rooted and grounded in the Covenant and objective reality.

Although my friend and I grew up in entirely different

environments and in ideological worlds apart, we have the same objective world view as if we had grown up together in the same family. That family is the Covenant and a worldwide nation of Jews and Gentiles. It is a nation defined by objective reality, founded on the supremacy of God as opposed to the supremacy of man. It is a nation not defined by race, language, a particular culture or geographic location but by the common grace of God and God's creation. It is a life and life- cultural manifestation of objective reality in creation. This is the human reality that was long ago articulated in the Bible. It is not elitism or an alternate of anything; it is the obligation and requirement to be objective and truthful about everything.

I have heard Iranian parents complain that they send their children to university, and they come back indoctrinated with radical Islam. Here in the West, the same thing happens. Our children go to university and often come back indoctrinated with radical liberal, Marxist and pagan ideologies.

In the Netherlands prior the Second World War, many of the Dutch were Nazi collaborators. They believed that getting on the good side of the Germans would help them get good jobs and advancements in the new world order. In other words, go proactive with the flow for your personal advancement. I call them Germans here because at this point, Nazism was main-stream and the only identity a German could have. This is not because I blame Germans for Nazism but because it illustrates the power ideology can have over people. We should also be aware that Nazism arose as a response to something.

It is because we fall for these things that we so often find ourselves on the wrong side of history. Ideology can never make a falsehood true or an alternate reality real. It destroys itself in derangement, and in the process causes major human suffering. It is this that is the wrong side of history.

We need major repentance and a return to the Covenant. Is global cooperation rooted in objective reality too much to ask for?

This is the twenty-first century; we have more than three thousand years of history to learn from - to teach us.

Another major threat to world peace today is Critical Race Theory- an ideological construct from American academia. It is very much similar to Critical Nation Theory of the twentieth century - one that caused two World wars and the holocaust; this one when allowed to continue may prove to be an even greater tragedy.

Most of you probably have experience the effect of critical race theory by being put down and accused of things you didn't even know and that are simply untrue. All of it is negative- intended to make you feel bad - that is my experience - this whole book is about it.

Critical Race Theory is an ideological construct of jurisprudence relying on moral relativism and social constructionism that has no standard of truth. It categorizes race, law and power. It equalized race with social behaviour, its structures, its cultural behaviour and its structures; Race is then defined as behaviour, culture, feelings and belief- and then also adds to this - standing in law and power - it effectively becomes a power structure to replace human rights.

It is a toxic mix intended to drive people against each other.

How do they get to this? Through an Ideological evaluation system employing the following - notions - Storytelling, naming one's own reality, intersectional theory, essentialism vs. anti-essentialism, Structural determinism, revisionist interpretations, empathic fallacy, non-white cultural nationalism/separatism, white privilege. I won't define all of these for you in this book - you can research them on your own - but I think the message is clear. The rule of Law and justice becomes notions and storytelling.

When race is defined like this - then it is not just about the African American or any other race - but much more about every possible behaviour, feeling and belief given standing in power and law. When everything is defined as the equivalency of race nothing could be wrong except the race. Any real attempt at solving any remaining racial issues is lost on ideological over reach by an ideology that clearly has begun ethic cleansing and is the pre-preparation for genocide.

The last time I have seen such Ideological social constructionism was in Nazi Germany- to construct the Aryan supper race and us as something less and Jews the scum of the world, the holocaust the final solution. It's astonishing, that American and western academia could fall this low.

This stands in stark contrast to the Covenant of Grace. This Ideology is an attempt to over throw the Covenant, Constitutional Government, Human Rights, Civil Liberty, and The Common Grace. It's an attempt to overthrow God – (the ban on human sacrifice, the foundation of human rights and righteousness in Justice). These concepts derive from the attributes of God, without them civil government and democracy are impossible.

As a reminder of what critical race theory can do you need to consider these facts. In western Europe during the Nazi occupation 71 percent of the Dutch Jews were deported and killed in the Holocaust, this may be less than in Poland, where 90 percent were killed but still much more than the 44 percent of German Jews and 25 percent of French Jews. Why were the Dutch Jews so vulnerable? There are a few distinct reasons for it that began right at the beginning of the Nazi occupation in the Netherlands. At the very beginning of the occupation Jews were told to register with the new Nazi Government as Jews and have their passports stamped with a J for identification as a Jew. The Dutch Jews dutifully complied. They believed compliance would produce the most favourable outcome. They were complacent – the product of living in a country where you could generally trust everyone and your government - they could not believe things could ever become as bad as they did. Those that will kill you come to you and speak to you as social workers - they are masters of deception - a deception that in time became very cruel. The Dutch Jews should have refused – ignored the request – take it as a warning - and as much as possible dispersed themselves throughout the country as Dutch, when at a time the Nazi occupiers were in no position to deport anyone. What this experience has etched on my mind is never co-operate with the ideology of any government.

Now to return to COVID-19 and its global impact now that we are six weeks into the lockdown and have gained some knowledge to give an opinion and ask for an end to this lockdown.

The first thing we need to do is remind ourselves that to live require taking a risk on death. Not wanting to take this risk is not having a life. This does not make a person reckless and irresponsible; that would be to tempt God. Nor should we be overly cautious or fearful, believing we need to control and micro-manage every environment. That is also in contempt of God and unrealistic. We are biological creatures living in an ecosystem, a part of that ecology, and with a rational mind.

A virus is a paradox. We don't want to get sick. We need to get immunity to the virus - we need to get to the other side of the virus. How do we get there? We should not pretend to have all the answers; neither should we blame others for the choices they make.

We were told at the outset of this virus threat that the lockdown, which began March 6, 2020, was to flatten the curve of infection of the virus that it would not overwhelm the healthcare system. Predictions were made of hundreds of thousands of deaths. Death rates were given of 5 per cent, 4 per cent, and 3 per cent of those infected. We accepted the lockdown, not knowing what to answer since we have no experience with this new virus. We now know from these six weeks the death rate from this virus is much lower than what was first portrayed. It does not appear to be much different from the past SARS virus and the Hong Kong flu.

I always see the daily statistics of COVID-19 infections and deaths. These statistics are only meaningful when compared to the control statistics. That would be a year without COVID-19. For example, in 2018, there were twenty-three deaths per 100,000 people in Canada from influenza A and influenza B. According to Statista. com reports that the death rate for influenza and pneumonia in Canada ranges from 16.1 to 23 deaths per 100,000 over the period of 2000 to 2018. This includes the 2008–2010 pandemic of H1N1 influenza. Then what death rate constitutes the designation of a pandemic requiring a social and economic lockdown? When do we decide that just protecting the vulnerable is sufficient? We need to see comparative statistics of all these deaths for the duration of the COVID-19 pandemic in order to make an objective opinion on the severity of this pandemic.

During the past SARS pandemic there was no lockdown or social distancing. We did what we could to protect those who were most vulnerable, the elderly and those with underlying health issues.

In the 1980 flu season, my wife was working in a nursing home that became infected despite precautions. Nine residents, or 12 per cent of the total residents, died that winter. It was a hard winter for staff, residents, and their families. However sad it might be, we understand that when you get old and weak, you might die from something that otherwise might be considered minor. My wife and I probably became infected, but we were never tested and not affected by the virus.

Today, reported COVID-19 deaths again come mostly from the elderly and those with underlying health issues. They are still not adequately protected if that was the goal in flattening the curve with the lockdown.

I also lived through the Hong Kong flu pandemic of 1968 and 1969. In 1969 I traveled with my parents to the Netherlands, which was apparently in the middle of the pandemic. When we were back in Canada, I became sick with the flu and then pneumonia. I could hardly breathe, and I thought I was going to die. I recovered on antibiotics and was not hospitalized. I was just fourteen then. I was the only one in our family who got sick, or at least very sick. No one told me it was the Hong Kong Flu. It was just the flu, and I was really sick.

For the Hong Kong flu there were no lockdown or social distancing rules. The flu was a health issue, not a political one. If you thought you were vulnerable for the flu, you protected yourself.

The Woodstock rock concert of August 1968, in Bethel, New York, was also held amid the Hong Kong flu pandemic. This was the rage and beginning of liberal progressivism. Politicians who are now putting us into lockdown may have been there. What has happened to progressivism? Are they now snowflakes? Or has progressivism now grown up? Do they want us to be snowflakes? The message from progressivism is confusing. Granted, at the beginning of the COVID-19 pandemic, we may not have known what this virus was. But I'm not so positive about that either; they have their research. In 1968, the progressives held a rock concert during a pandemic with no social distancing. Today you may not have a church service, not even with social distancing.

In the past six weeks of lockdown I hardy used a tank of fuel in my pickup. Twenty years ago, I was nearly killed in a traffic accident. That experience did not discourage me from driving. If this lockdown would last forever, the risk for any future accident would almost be eliminated. Am I to consider that a benefit? As a small business owner I know, we cannot survive the effects of lockdowns or partial lockdowns on business loans and debts that need to be repaid.

We need to end the lockdown and allow people to go to their churches, work, and schools. For any future pandemic, we need to isolate the source as a first response, and we need cooperation from them at the source; after that, and if that fails, we need to protect the vulnerable among us.

We have a right to choose. We can choose to protect ourselves if we think that is in our best interests, even if it is until there is a vaccine. We also have the right to take the risk of herd immunity. The sooner we establish immunity, the safer it becomes for the vulnerable. And no one can be forced to be vaccinated. All of this is part of our civil liberties.

What then is our problem that requires such a dramatic response? When China has a particular political response to a health problem, does the whole world need to follow suit and its format? How do we know that China was not trying to contain a virus research accident to prevent embarrassment and liability? That becomes more apparent with their suspicious behaviour; they are not helping themselves with such behaviour. Was this virus possibly thought to be an enhanced potential pandemic pathogen (EPPP)? In 2019 the research in EPPP was again commenced in the United States after being paused for many years (*Science,* February 8, 2019). This is the research conducted by the virologists Yoshihiro Kawaoka of the University of Wisconsin-Madison and Ron Fouchier from the Netherlands, Erasmus Medical Center. In 2012 they intentionally developed a virus strain based on the H5N1 virus for which no vaccine exists. This caused outrage in both the media and scientific community. There is no reason to believe that China put such research on hold.

An article in *Science* (February 8, 2019) quoted Harvard University epidemiologist Mark Lipsitch commenting on the restart of the research: "We are now being asked to trust a completely opaque process where the outcome is to permit the continuation of dangerous experiments."

EPPP research is dual-use technology. It can be used to create the viral disease and then the patented vaccine for the virus. This might be a very good for-profit business plan but very unethical. The second useful purpose is to create weapons of mass destruction. The excuse offered to justify the research is to get a better understanding of pandemics and their control.

We know from history that after 1650, the Indigenous population of North America was decimated by European viruses such as smallpox and measles. This genocidal possibility can now be replicated with EPPPs for the entire world. In theory, with the right virus and right vaccine, holocaust population control becomes possible.

People of the world are being put on edge and becoming fearful of any virus, as well as with the knowledge of EPPPs. The fear itself is menacing. This has become especially and noticeably acute with the progressive ideological elite concerning COVID-19. I would like to know why. The threat of EPPPs is a violation of our human rights and civil liberties. Ideology should not be in control of science and healthcare. Any state that engages in this research of EPPPs and biological weapons should be put under quarantine with a travel ban and a trade ban. The people of the world require protection from this threat.

Global media and communication

Probably another great threat to the people of the present world is our reliance on internet media; its use, its control, and its possible lose.

In 2011, during the financial crisis we had demonstrations and protests on Wall Street, New York City and other cities around the world, protesting the 1%,(the supper rich), blaming them for the financial crisis. These protesters were pathetic and showed they had no comprehension of what they were protesting, and now, neither do the present day protesters. It is astonishing how in 2020 and 2021 the ideological Marxist mob appears to be supporting the 1% and destroying their own neighborhoods, at least for the moment. It also appears the 1% is learning how to manage the media and social media to control or direct the mob for their benefit.

To make a few comments on the current social media crisis; I hardly use social media, I only use it to get information from certain sites, ones I like that are on these platforms. I don't use it to construct feelings, emotions, or passions. I don't use twitter neither parler. I'll give you my reasons.

Social media was created by some high school students. The system setup reflects adolescent high school culture. The method of communication is very deficient. It is very heavy on evoking emotions and very shallow in communicating knowledge. Using hash-tags, likes, unlikes, mojes, short catalyst messages, trolling, doxing, threats, even death threats, funnel all of this through personalized media feeds and you may get a very concentrated toxic brew, enough to drive anyone to derangement. We should not take social media so serious. Before social media all these things could go nowhere, they went into the ground, now stupidity can be amplified and go to the top of the world. Unfortunately it could be dangerous, derangement is unpredictable.

Social media may appear benign but it has become a high speed barbaric Stone Age method of communicating. All this made into billions of dollars worth of business. We should quit social media and find different ways to keep contact. We need to diversify, that includes go back to what we did before internet, then we had memberships in civil organizations that network together across the entire country, and that could also do on ground community work, and at the same time influence the state. We need to expand our base for the Covenant in our communities and especially in our inner-cities. There is also a great need to Work on election integrity in our local communities and states. It appears that our third branch of government, when it comes to election integrity is full of dithering Judges. Allowing the unverifiable and unaccountable to stand as legitimate is in its self the defrauding of the voter.

The founders of these media platforms now realize they have created a beast; and now would like to tame the beast? To change the platforms into an ideological publishing house to edit and censor users does not solve the problem. When people want to put themselves into ideological boxes where they can beat-up on straw men, that is their problem, but I won't join them. Such activity leads to the encouragement of pogroms.

I call it a beast. You need to consider what happened on social media, in the US presidential election of 2016. The media attack on Donald Trump and his supporters was severe and relentless, that only accelerated after he was elected president. You can expect people to defend themselves against these attacks and that it will accelerate as well in time. In the end with the presidential election of 2020, it was Trump supporters and Trump himself that got censored, shadow band and them completely band form social media platforms. You couldn't take it any longer. It's you, Trump haters and the owners of these platforms that are the poor losers. It is adolescent behaviour gone mad. You all need to grow up. What social media did in censoring one political party; I consider a crime against the people affected and against our constitutional democracy. It's an issue for criminal and civil law.

Today I am expected to use internet for my business, commercial business and personal business as well. For this I need access to a platform, it has become a necessity in order to participant in the economy and the state. Then it has also become a right. Then for this I need a public platform that is governed by the state's criminal law and civil law, that I may have the protection of the law. I will operate my business within the confines of the rule of law and justice, but I will not have my business censored, edited or shadow band by a publisher I can do that myself, or I can chose my publisher, again within the confines of civil and criminal justice.

To clean up the internet platforms we need to enforce criminal and civil law. We need to adapt a branch of justice specific for internet crimes that is fast, inexpensive and easily accessible by the average person. Something like a small- claims court, as the starting point.

When we are expected to use internet and it becomes a necessity, then we also need consumer choice; it's time to break up the monopoly of big tech. Big tech only has the business because the consumers are willing to use the product and has the knowledge to use it even to the point where they don't like it. Business is not a one-way street it is reciprocal. A civil economy and State includes and protects the consumer.

9

THE MONETARY COVENANT

Probably the most misunderstood phenomenon in the world and one that leaves most people feeling helpless is understanding money. Nevertheless, I ask you to question the validity of conventional monetary policy and to make a choice: Could there be such a thing as a monetary Covenant? What have we got today?

I first began to write about this after the Wall Street protest in 2011 in New York City. The protestors did not know what they were demonstrating for or against. Just being unhappy about something does not solve the problem. But it might encourage some people to think and write about it.

I read several books by supposed experts on globalism. They all began their books by trying to put globalism into a historic perspective, but right here at the beginning, they failed. They had no clue about the history of money or religion and its effects on human development.

The problem is not with the banks, lending money, and the economy. All of these can be regulated by an objective rule of law and justice, and they should be regulated. The real problem is with money itself and monetary policy as money becomes a law of itself.

Prior to the mortgage crises in the United States in 2008, your house may have been valued at $200,000 resale value. In 2020, the retail value may be $600,000 to $800,000. This is not wealth; it is mostly monetary attrition. We can again leverage this attrition with borrowing to spend in the economy, which will inevitably happen when the house is sold. Stimulating growth in the economy while, at the same time, our children are finding out they cannot afford to buy a house. There is a problem with the monetary system.

Once we realized it was a crisis in 2008, interest rates were dropped severely or to zero in order to encourage buying and to stimulate the economy. However, this money, suddenly available at almost no interest, did not come from your or my savings (maybe some from China). It was all quantitative easing, created money. In effect, it was increasing consumer debt on attrition as the collateral to flood out past debt with more debt. This does not solve the problem; it just puts some life back into the problem until a future crisis. Again the problem is with monetary policy.

If this is how we solved the monetary crisis brought on by the mortgage defaults, why could we not have used the same method combined with higher equity requirements to prevent it from happening in the first place? It would have prevented misery for a lot of people.

How do we know that this quantitative easing was adequate or excessive for the purpose? What is its real benefit? Isn't the greatest benefit for global capitalists rather than for the people? Billionaires are having billions more added to their billions through the attrition of money in relation to their assets.

What about those people saving towards buying a house? It just puts a home that much farther out of reach. And what of those who are renting a house or apartment? Do we just give them rental increases? Is participation in the state now only for those who own property?

During the monetary crisis in Europe, Germany was trying to impose austerity measures on Greece, Italy, and Spain in an attempt to maintain value for monetary assets. However, the people of these countries were electing to government some very strong opposition to Germany and austerity. Austerity began to look like it would be suicide for the EU. As a result, austerity fell off the face of the earth;

we never heard of it again. It was quickly replaced with quantitative easing. Again the problem is not solved.

Here in Canada, where I live and hence am more familiar, I have heard the same partisan economic, monetary rhetoric all my life. The Liberals want to fund everything, deficit spending, and debt accumulation. Conservatives say they will balance the budget and reduce the debt. This has been political rhetoric as long as I can remember, for at least fifty years. Debt keeps accumulating to increase the money supply, and attrition (devaluation) keeps moving forward. This political rhetoric has lost all credibility. It is astonishing that it is still being repeated, always threatening that a future generation will need to pay. Actually we are that generation and are paying for it through attrition.

Today everyone knows that debt is paid by the creation of more debt, especially with public debt. When debt is paid with debt and debt can never be paid without drying up the money supply, then why is it debt? Debt that cannot be paid has no value. Then again, why is it debt?

I think today's international monetary system is a function of a whole lot of incompetence that can be navigated to achieve monetary conquest.

Today, with the COVID-19 pandemic, everything has changed again, requiring a massive amount of created money to support a large shift in consumerism, where all the focus is on emergency healthcare, and economic shutdown. Is this then all more debt that needs to be repaid in the future?

I will try to find the evidence to support a monetary Covenant that will include the people in the creation of monetary wealth, from the history of money.

History of Money

The use of coins as money began in history almost as soon as metals were discovered and could be processed. They were added to the barter trade. The discovery of gold and silver, although not very useful for utensils or implements, had a special quality that was appreciated by everyone. It naturally became the product to impress, jewellery to express wealth and then money.

The only purpose of money is to secure payment, as the ancient Hebrew word for payment indicates *t'shalom,* "to make peace," or to requite. This can be achieved through simple bartering, agreeing on goods for goods or services for services. But this barter system can never work well for complex transactions or any major projects requiring the cooperation from many people. Coins of precious metals overcame this problem.

However, coins in themselves are still nothing regardless of the metal. Their ability to have any value for payment—or making peace—lies completely in the consciousness of the human being. Subjectively, human beings were impressed by the aesthetic quality of gold and silver to the point that they coveted gold and silver. It became an objective a priori and could become a universal law of payment, accepted by friend and foe alike. Payments could now be expressed in weights of precious metals as human covetousness guaranteed universal acceptance (confidence). The world then had one universal currency with real purchasing power. And herein already lies the problem with money. The universal law of payment relies on covetousness and, at the same time, is expected to be moral for making payment.

Now who creates money, purchasing power? Throughout history it was whoever found gold and silver as the primary source. A secondary source is capital accumulation through mercantile trade, and also through taxation by government. From here we get into monetarism, where capital is lent out at interest to mercantile trade, industry, agriculture, government, and anyone who may have the ability to make interest and principal payments. However, despite this debt, it is always the original non-debt supply of gold and silver that determines the total supply of purchasing power. Much of our history is defined according to the supply of gold and silver.

We should keep in mind that historically money is intended to make peace and payment, a moral and priori law. It is great irony in the world's history to see what we have done to each other in order to acquire tokens of peace and payment.

Today we have fiat money. The American dollar was removed from the gold standard in 1971. Money no longer has a reference to gold; the real value of money is public confidence. The quantity of money is controlled by math. In other words, numerical units that can continue to infinity. Money comes into existence only through debt. The supply and demand for money is to be controlled by manipulating interest rates, and as you see today, that is hardly possible.

Now a few examples of monetary problems from history. In ancient Mesopotamia and the Middle East, after about 1,500 BC, the land was settled by small city-states and nomads. These states had functioning economies that included farming, industry, and trade. Money was in use, yet there were constant petty wars between these states. These wars were carried out to acquire wealth and power beyond what existing economics could produce. Another factor that should not be overlooked is the contempt for each other's ideology (religion), a feeling of deficiency in truth and justice.

An account of one of these petty wars can be found in Genesis 34, when Jacob's sons were confronted with the problem of their sister Dinah and the proposed marriage to Shechem. Hamor and his son Shechem thought they had a merger with Jacob's family through marriage. However, Jacob's sons had a different idea; they killed all the men and took the women and children, cattle, and money. They made it into an economic stimulus package for themselves.

Another good example from the Bible that illustrates monetary deficiency is from the account of King Solomon and the State of

Israel. We read that King Solomon sent ships to get gold from Ophir. New gold from an outside source wins the right to expand the money supply and receives the initial benefit of economic stimulus. At the end of Solomon's reign, we read of no more new gold but instead of high taxes and the kingdom falling apart. It is probable that through trade and consumerism, the economy was dispossessed of gold for capital accumulation, which was taken to another state, where it would be used to expand that economy. What was needed for Israel was another shipment of new gold. Increasing the money supply could have provided the economic stimulus to rescue the state, but that did not happen.

Nothing in the economy of the State of Israel was lacking other than money. Money is the only means to facilitate the operations of a complex economy. The only other means is by draconian rule of law, the difference between willing cooperation and unwilling cooperation. The real problem was the monetary leakage. The only way to recover money outside of a primary source is through trade, war, or by surrendering sovereignty to another state who could promise money.

All through the middle Ages we have the same scenario for Western Europe, beginning in the second or third century. The Roman super-rich hoarded the supply of money and land, keeping the people in debt, poverty, and slavery. Then this monetary system from the crumbling Roman Empire simply transferred to the feudal rulers and the Roman Catholic church. Then the next thousand years became a time of economic stagnation and a short money supply .The only times the money supply expanded were in preparation for war and the building of castles and cathedrals. Then it was soon taxed back.

This system only began to break up when there were more free people and some trade. However, the real breakthrough did not come until Spain unified and then conquered Granada and then discovered America. In America they conquered the Aztecs, Mayans, and Incas, stole their gold, and brought it back to Europe, thereby winning the right to expand the money supply for themselves and all of Europe. For once in a thousand years there was a substantial increase in the money supply, and this time not all of it was in the control of the feudal system or the church. Much of the gold stayed in the hands of the conquistadors and their families and used for discretionary spending and investment.

Now why would Spain have a monopoly over the expansion of the money supply? There were not too many in Europe who agreed. We have Sir Francis Drake from England and Piet Hein from the Netherlands who made it their business to rob Spanish treasure ships. Sir Francis Drake was knighted for his successful efforts by Queen Elizabeth the first of England; did they do any crime? Spain could very well have become the banking centre of the world, but they destroyed that opportunity with their Ideology. The Roman Catholic church would not allow lending money for interest. And then add to this the persecution of Protestants and Jews by the Jesuit Spanish inquisition. The banking centre moved to Amsterdam in the Netherlands, a country that was a refuge for the persecuted of Europe and where Jews were equal citizens.

We often think that the Renaissance, Reformation, and Enlightenment were spontaneous events, but I think they were very much aided through the monetary expansion from private sources outside the direct control of the established tyranny. It provided the means and courage for individuals to exert themselves, but also for the moneyed network to sustain reform.

More recently in North America, it is often said the American West was developed through the California gold rush. It is more accurate to say the American West was developed through the creation of new capital money—purchasing power—and gold was the capitalists' excuse.

Now back to Europe. In the time when Western Europe was in the Dark Ages, the eastern half of the old Roman Empire, the Byzantine Empire, continued for another thousand years. They had a larger population, an adequate gold supply, and a stable currency for the first eight hundred years. They had a free-enterprise economy controlled by the rule of law. Trade was regulated, and every attempt was made to replace imports with home production. They had a large middle class and no super-rich, but the state as a whole was very wealthy. It only came to an end through constant attacks of war by Islam and no reliable ally from Western Europe.

The historic model for Western capitalism is without any doubt the ancient Greeks. In Greece, the land itself was not prosperous in terms of agriculture or food production. Supporting a population required sea trade and colonization around the Mediterranean there they were able to build advanced city-states. This advanced development of these city-states could not have been achieved through a barter economy. The Greeks had gold and silver mines; mining was an important occupation for the Greeks.

It was through Greek trade that an ever-increasing supply of money as wealth was introduced into the Mediterranean region. For the first time in European history, portable wealth, gold and silver as money, became more important than the wealth of land.

The Greek city-states and colonies were attacked by Persia in wars beginning in 490 BC. Territory was lost to Persia, and gold was redirected to Persia.

During these wars, the Athenians discovered a rich vein of silver in Laurium in about 480 BC. In the Athens assembly, under the leadership of Themistocles, it was proposed by Aristides and his supporters that the silver be divided and distributed among all the citizens in the same manner as the spoils of war. Themistocles instead insisted that the new wealth be used to build a strong fleet of at least two hundred additional warships in preparation for the next Persian sea invasion. Aristides was ostracized—voted out—from the assembly for ten years, and the money went to build the ships. All this money was newly created purchasing power, not debt as no one owed anyone anything.

What is clear from this history is that new purchasing power as money came into existence through the people as individual citizens and collectively as the community. Greek citizens could purchase their leisure lives with newly created purchasing power, and none of this was debt. They owed no one anything. Instead, through colonization and lending money, the world came to owe them. At the same time, it should be remembered that the majority who lived in Athens during this time were not citizens, and this would not apply to them. Slavery is also an aspect of the monetary system. By keeping productive people from participating in the money economy, it protects the supply of money for those who have it.

The Persian's navy of King Xerxes was defeated in a major sea battle in 480 BC. His navy went home. After this, the Greek city-states formed a formal federation for defence. This federation did not work but caused a war. While the city-states squabbled and fought each other, King Philip II of Macedonia consolidated his state in the north. He seized the northern gold mines, thereby depriving the southern city-states a good portion of their money supply.

This money from these mines was diverted to Macedonia and used to build a new navy and army for the state. In light of the contemporary time, this was a new and innovative high-tech navy and army. When you have enough money and everyone gets paid well, you can buy a lot of cooperation from the people. Again this is all primary money; created purchasing power, not debt or war bonds; King Philip owed no one anything.

With this army and navy, King Philip II conquered all the Greek city-states; destroyed democracy, and made himself tyrant of all Greece, himself, the one and only citizen.

After the death of King Philip, his son, Alexander, became king. He took this new army to attack Persia to regain lost territory and get revenge on the previous Persian attacks. This conquest was funded with gold and silver from the mines, not by debt or war bonds. And when this was not enough, the spoils of conquest would provide the rest.

Alexander conquered the Persian Empire in eleven years with four major battles. After the Battle of Issus, he took the city of

Damascus and there apprehended the Persian war treasury, gaining all new purchasing power to continue his conquest. The Persians lost their money to fund the war.

Alexander's empire did not last. It was divided into four kingdoms, and governance of a large empire with an inadequate money supply was difficult. However, the sequence of money and debt, how it has evolved, continues according to this pattern to our modern time. It is clear from this history that capitalism cannot exist without the creation of money that is wealth in its own, a commodity that has no reference to economic activity nor debt. Money as wealth in itself becomes the command of economic activity. It is a law in itself. Debt cannot be created without it, and money (purchasing power) created by debt is not this wealth.

The Gold Standard

Today there are still some people who think we should return to the gold standard. Most people today agree that the depression of the 1930s was caused by the gold standard, and if it had not been for the gold standard, the Depression could have been prevented. The world's gold supply is inadequate, and the means by which it came into existence as money is much less than desirable.

With the gold standard, money was created by lending to the public on a ratio of gold reserve held by the bank. This system works as long as no one asks for their gold. When everyone asks for their gold, you will soon find out that most of your money is not gold but, rather, someone else' debt. With fiat money, the system is still the same but without reference to gold. The reserve is expressed in a quantity of money that can be increased or decreased by restrictive lending (taking in more than letting out), a bond (loan) from the central bank, or quantitative easing. (In reference to history, this would be the same as new gold coming from a mine.) Now, all primary capital is held by the central bank or the reserve. There is no longer any primary capital with the people, like gold coming into circulation as money from a private source. All money in circulation is someone's else' debt, and therefore private enterprise's capital accumulation can only be the debt accumulation of someone else.

The problem with debt money is that it always requires future economic activity in order to repay. Primary money is capital purchasing power that does not require future economic activity. It is wealth in itself.

Gold Method

I think it is clear from history that for a very long time, money came into existence and circulated as primary capital money by anyone who could produce it. As in the example of the Greek city-states, primary capital reserve money was distributed by democratic means to its citizens. Today, with fiat money, I see no reason why this could not be done again to correct the imbalance between capital money and debt money. At the same time, we would need to restrict the growth of debt to maintain the balance.

Inherent Value of Money

Historically, the value of money was focused on gold, the metal, as a tradable commodity. However, the real value that became apparent is its usefulness as purchasing power. Then it follows, the context that makes money most useful to the citizen is social, economic, political stability that can also be characterized by reliable and objective justice, human rights, and the rule of law. These properties are the true value of money. A democratic state that has these properties in place may create as much primary capital money as it needs for its citizens from time to time as the economy may require.

Free Trade

From ancient times states and economies got sacked, stripped of their assets and money for the purpose of enriching the raider or conqueror. Nothing much has changed; we still do the same thing, only in a modern way and without gold. Where everything is financialized, the sacking is put on a promissory note for a future generation. And when that generation comes, we have a financial crisis. We do this within the state, through government deficit spending, and now globally with the financing of trade and capital imbalances, creating economic imbalances and the debt trap of nations around the world.

Now the question: Do trade and deficits need to be balanced if money and debt are to have any value? Adam Smith, author of *The Nature and Cause of Wealth of Nations* (1796) is considered to be the cornerstone of neo-Liberal economics. (I have heard reports that Prime Minister Margaret Thatcher of England always kept a copy in her purse; she loved it.) If we are to get anything out of Smith's ideas, we need to update them. His writing is not pure philosophy but pure reason applied to his time. In Smith's time, the world was still a large frontier; much of it was hardly explored. Money was gold and silver. There were many new mines that produced a steady supply of gold and silver, all entering the monetary system and being loaned for interest to the point that there was inflation. Today the world looks more like a fishbowl. With fiat money, there is no primary source of money coming from within the economy, only debt money from a presupposed capital reserves held in the central banking system.

Adam Smith considered labour to be the major component of price. That may have been true for his day, when it required a lot of labour to manufacture or produce anything. However, with today's technology, labour is becoming the smallest component in pricing. Billionaires have become billionaires by downsizing corporations and exporting our jobs to Communist China, capitalism taking advantage of its labour laws.

Adam Smith envisioned that trade imbalances would correct themselves through competition and improved productivity— the invisible hand, or in the French Revolutionary terms, laissez faire. But instead we have the financialization of trade and capital imbalances, and then with fiat money, on the a priori of math, this can continue to infinity. We may have free trade, but the trade wars have only been transferred to monetary wars, capital wars, and fiscal wars. Someone needs to call a judgement on value, and that should be the people. They are the ones paying the price with lost jobs and lost incomes.

What do we mean by competition and improved productivity to equalize trade? According to Smith, the equalizing trade that would result can only be through the equalizing of the price for goods. The price for goods consists of three components: a return on capital, a return on labour, and a return for government in the form of tax. All three of these need equalizing to balance trade under a free-trade policy. Adam Smith's concept is inadequate to equalize anything, much less strategic goods such as oil. However, concerning price, when there is very little labour input or labour cost and no taxes, how then do you equalize profit and the return on intellectual property or resource property? It can only happen when we force it to happen through import taxes in the importing state or through higher wages, human rights, and Social Security in the exporting state. Without this equalizing, we create production states and consumer states as the new divisions of labour, and the absurdity of fiat money as wealth continues our debt. Through this type of unmitigated division of labour, the consumer in mature, developed economies still remains a component of labour for income but without any representation in the price structure. Much of our consumer debt is a shortfall in the labour component of price, debt; it's a substitute for real income. With short-sighted consumerism, more consumption and capital accumulation can be achieved through consumer debt than with higher prices, prices that would include a civil value for labour. The efficiency of production is worthless to the consumer and producer when it cannot include the consumer as a source of income through labour, value added, or dividends. In other words, the benefit of lower prices is not income for the people. Efficiency should be for the benefit of the entire economy, not just for lower prices and capital accumulation for billionaires.

Adam Smith also stated in *The Nature and Cause of Wealth of Nations*, "all production is for consumption." If that is true, then it cannot be for surplus capital accumulation. This can only be possible when we deny that a portion of consumption has taken place and defer it to another time, which is represented by consumer and government debt. By comparison, much of eighteenth-century capital was surplus gold from the mines and colonies, not debt.

When production does not need labour, there is a moral obligation to include the welfare of the consumer—the population—in the price structure through value added. Without this, production is not sustainable. People do not need to be unemployed. But we need to direct labour away from the waste of consumerism and towards environmental/economic stewardship. Environmental protection must be inserted into the price and economic structure to replace the labour component that was lost. Like I said before, efficiency belongs to the entire economy, not just for lower prices and capital accumulation.

Neo-Liberal economics make their defence from Adam Smith and his eighteenth-century experience in trade to defend their doctrine of free trade, no taxes, and floating exchange rates to balance trade and capital flows. However, the eighteenth-century idea of money is quite different from today's. Adam Smith had a rather casual idea of money. He writes, "The cheapness of gold and silver render those metals rather less fit for the purposes of money than they were before." In other words, trade and industrial expansion has to catch up to the money supply if money was to retain any value, and this flow of money continued year after year. This is all primary capital money, no one's debt.

As the economic activity of the nineteenth century caught-up to the money supply and gold was no longer so plentiful, money was created through debt on the gold base.

Then in the twentieth century, money was removed from the gold standard and was created through debt based on the reserve in the banking system, a presupposed reserve of the central bank.

Obviously in the eighteenth century, every advantage for trade and economic development was with the state that had access to cheap gold and silver from the mines or colonies. It is easy to promote free trade when you are speaking from this advantage. States that did not have access to cheap gold and silver could only obtain it through trade or debt.

Now apply this recent history to our fiat money policy. The challenge is to get the currency of one dominant state, or a few states, to be accepted as the world currency of trade and debt, and thereby, all other currencies become secondary. States with secondary currencies will be required to use the currency of the dominant state to complete trade transactions and seek investments. These currencies are being crowded out, as the dominant currency takes on the characteristics that once were attributed to gold. Therefore, these smaller states lose the ability to create their own reserves or primary sources of money for investment and trade. The dominant states become the only source of primary money or reserves. In eighteenth-century terms, they would have the only gold mine in the world, at least for creating purchasing power, and all other states would be dependent on that state for a money supply. Economic development only becomes possible through trade and capital flows, not through the states' own abilities to create money. That ability now belongs only to the dominant state or states.

Once the dominant state has the world flooded with its money and its economy operating reasonably well, it can start raising interest rates and thereby collect tribute from the whole world, causing economic stress in other states, which in turn, provide the justification to micro-manage the affairs of these states. This is today's attempt at imperialism, monetary absolutism providing social credit and welfare for capitalism, debt, and servility for the world and its people.

We need to develop a monetary system that will make local, regional, and national economies more self-sufficient and self-reliant. This should be the new consciousness for globalism. The tools to do this are local control of monetary policy, fiscal policy, and the people's primary capital money. Global capital markets can never achieve this. Instead, they create dependency and regional disparity as well as tsunamis of capital flows as we have seen with the past Asian monetary crisis.

We need a monetary system where we can contract the economy and, at the same time, preserve prosperity, improve the quality of life and protect the environment. The present system of ever-increasing consumption and waste to maintain growth for the purpose of staying ahead of debt with more debt money is not sustainable but will end in a tyranny. It already has—debt tyranny. We need to reduce consumption and debt. That can only be achieved through the use of the people's primary capital money, a dividend on economic efficiency and objective justice, including real human rights.

The people of each state in the world could create their own capital and then would not be dependent on global capital markets. If each state used the same criteria, we in essence would have one global currency. We need to replace monetary imperialism with the monetary imperative, which is not unlike the moral imperative. They are the same.

The present monetary system can never achieve this as it emphasizes the wrong end of the economic process. It will carry on from crisis to crisis, each time mitigated by attrition. We are all beginning to realize that money has no real value other than being the pretext for conquest.

10

CONCLUSION

Is there a positive foundation for monetary policy to be discovered from our history? Is there a moral foundation for monetary policy? Is there a biblical foundation for monetary policy? After all, the Bible is history as well as moral concepts and justice. Monetary policy and economics may not be the theme of the Bible, but it is a part of it that may be more important than we think. The Bible is very clear on holistic life concepts in justice and history.

To deduct a natural monetary policy from our history and the Bible, I highlight the most obvious that I have found. From this we should be able to draw a conclusion to solve our current and ongoing monetary crises. At least it should shine some clear light on it.

The Bible allows and assumes it to be relevant that gold and silver is money as payment and portable wealth. The Bible first mentions gold as possible portable wealth in Genesis 2 : 11:12 AKJV: "Havilah where there is Gold; and the gold of that land is good; there is bdellium and the onyx stone."

The next most obvious that I can observe is that the moral law, justice, and the Covenant, as they are given from God, are far above gold in value. I think Psalm 19 AKJV expresses this quite well. "The fear of the Lord is clean, enduring for ever: the judgments of the Lord are true and righteous altogether. More to be desired are they than gold, yea than much fine gold:"

Then we find that various places in the Bible rebuke excessive debt and interest rates.

I think this may describe the basics that can be known from the Bible. For now I deal with these.

What I recognize here is that gold is never represented as debt, not in the Bible nor in our history. It comes into existence as money and wealth, as capital by anyone who can acquire it from its source, from the mines or by trade. Money is produced within the economy as a commodity of trade. It is only lent on debt with the anticipation that the supply will continue in the future, that it might be paid back. There is no regard for its source.

The moral law was known from the beginning and given to a nation from God by the hand of Moses. It was given to sinners as a rule for life for our own good. We, being sinners, are therefore debtors to the law. Understanding this from God's Word, the intention is to bring us to repentance and faith in God and salvation in Jesus Christ, all again confirming the value of the moral law. We might learn humility and recognize the supremacy of God and the rule of law for our own good.

How is any of this relevant to monetary policy? Whether you believe anything from the Bible or not, you might recognize that the human subjective must be a confirmation of objective reality for there to be any value for and from anything. In other words, in this world, true value for anything, including money, is only found through civil moral life, not just raw covetousness. This is why the Bible states that the moral law is esteemed more than gold; true value is established in a moral context.

Now compare this to what is at work in our day. How can today's monetary and economic positions be verified by our history and the Bible to be right or even good? And what does it prove to us?

As mentioned previously, money comes into existence only as debt and infrequently as "quantitative easing" from the Federal Reserve to the banks. Newly created money is lent and re-lent primarily to the people and government and then is spent in the economy. Over time, much of it becomes accumulated by the global capitalist elite as capital, which then is not debt. The poor get poorer, having most of the debt; the elite get richer, having most of the capital. The whole process of dispossession of the people is accelerated when mega corporations can borrow mega quantities of capital, including from quantitative easing through the banks at almost no interest, bypassing money markets (which today don't really exist anyway) for the purpose of dispossessing the people of their money and increasing the consumer debt.

Today we say the economy is good; everyone is working, and there is growth. However, this growth is animated by the quantitative easing of a few years ago to get the economy out of the monetary crisis of 2008 in the United States and Europe. It was the only option left seeing how politically dangerous austerity measures were becoming. This money has come into circulation by forcing up real estate prices, leveraging property to put more people deeper into debt, and expanding consumer debt. Our economic growth of today is on this leverage; it is actually attrition, the devaluation of our money. Does it cause inflation? Not much in consumer goods because there is no shortage of manufactured consumer goods and cheap labour provided by a totalitarian communist state. But in food and housing, inflation is significant. Publishing an accurate cost-of-living index has become unfashionable in our day with the elite.

President Donald Trump, with his America first trade policy and bringing back manufacturing, is trying to make sure much of the money from this quantitative easing, along with American jobs, stay in the United States to prevent this monetary crisis from happening again anytime soon. Eventually it will happen again. In the meantime, we may end up with a housing affordability crisis, especially when they increase interest rates.

We as an economy are accumulating debt that everyone knows will never get paid. We know we pay debt with more debt. When debt cannot be paid—and everyone knows this debt can never be paid—then why is it debt? Public debt is debt from the people that is owed to the people. Public debt should never be owed to a foreign power, and that is also why trade needs to be balanced. When we put ourselves in debt to foreign powers, we are selling our sovereignty. If any payment is to be expected outside of trade, then this is the only true value.

Now consider the ideological world and its direction towards the idea of justice. It can primarily be described as moral relativism. When there is no moral truth, then neither is there a debt to any moral law. The ideology is righteous, and the only sin is to violate that ideology.

This is the opposite of what we see in scripture, in our Bible, and also what we can find in our history. It is problematic seeing money is all about real and objective value. How can our ideological values ever be a sound foundation for monetary policy? How can it ever be a logical foundation for money or value for anything? How is moral relativism, ideology, and alternate realities a sound business plan or a foundation for monetary policy?

In ideology, money is debt for the other, the consumer. Moral obligation is for the other, outside the ideology. There is no reciprocity. The reciprocity between the consumer and producer is arrested by the dispossession of the consumer of his or her share of value (the individual's money) in the economy and is being replaced for the consumer with debt. We are denying that all production is for consumption and imagining that some of it is for monetary capital accumulation. This is why we keep accumulating more and more debt—and also have more and more billionaires.

Today we have a monetary system that is imperialist; it is repression and slavery; Enslaved to debt and to consumerism, a 24-7 economy motivated by debt that delivers stress and fear, with escape being offered as just one more consumer product. It can only continue by staying ahead of debt through creating more debt and more wasteful consumerism to accommodate or justify the debt. We know from the past that austerity measures are political suicide for governments because they are the causes of suffering for the people and will provoke protest, even revolution.

How do we break out of this cycle? My submission is this, based on these few facts from our history and how they relate to the Bible: Through the use of an asset-based monetary system and an asset-motivated economy, rather than the present debt-based monetary system and debt-motivated economy. The motivation to save should be just as strong as the motivation to spend.

We should establish a fourth branch of constitutional government called the monetary congress to replace the Federal Reserve. It would also bring new life and meaning to democracy. (I love constitutional democracies.) It would decide on the level of quantitative easing that may be needed each year, and the money would be sent directly to every citizen. It would be a dividend on economic efficiency and the capital of civil society. It may be subject to taxes from the government.

When businesses need to borrow capital, they will need to offer an attractive interest rate to attract their needed capital; we would once again have a meaningful money market. Debt would then also require a much higher reserve that it does today.

Asset money would be coming into the economy from within the economy in the same manner as gold entered the economy as money, as it has done so for thousands of years. Only this time, being fiat money, it will come by democratic means based on a constitutional or covenantal right found in universal objective justice—the supremacy of God and the rule of law.

If this congress created too much money, we might have inflation; if it did not create enough, we might have a recession. The allowable ratio of debt to asset for lending should also be reduced under this system. In this manner, asset-driven becomes meaningful and implemented.

The real foundation of fiat money, what gives it value, is the objective reliable justice of the state that issues the money, a justice system that recognizes objective human rights, not rights for ideology in order to discriminate. This foundation is the supremacy of God and the rule of law as understood from the biblical moral law, the requirement to be objective concerning creation and reality. This is the true definition for an honest secular or civil state.

From history we know that states with a justice system that gravitates towards objective truth and justice, a biblical foundation, become stable states and preferred states for the migration of people. Then it also follows that such a state would experience a stable currency brought about through preferred demand or confidence.

The stability of the issuing state becomes the foundation for the currency. This is not a debt; it is an asset. The currency of a state that is a tyranny with no objective justice and human rights should have no value for its currency in the world market. They cannot maintain the constitutional asset but are a liability.

A state with an objective justice system and human rights should be allowed to create its own currency, which should be accepted on par with similar currencies. In other words, developing and emerging countries may create their own foreign aid in as much as their growing economies can accommodate without being inflationary, providing they provide a stable objective justice system. This should be the first priority to sound monetary policy. These growth economies by expanding the money supply provid economic stimulation for established mature economies that may otherwise be downsizing; no economy needs to become stagnate.

Environmental cleanup could be implemented with created funds without stimulating consumption. At the same time, it would generate income, replacing income that otherwise would need to be generated through excessive consumerism. With this monetary system, consumerism can be reduced without reducing prosperity. It will have a net positive impact on the environment. An asset-driven economy will work to restore and protect the environment. A debt-driven economy seeks more growth in consumption in order to stay ahead of the growing debt and, therefore, is environmentally hostile because it encourages excessive consumer waste to continue producing growth. With this monetary system we cannot continue ignoring trade deficits or trying to use them as leverage on other states as we do in the current game of monetary and economic imperialism.

Trade should be balanced through trade agreements that include wage increases and price increases. The objective should be that each state becomes self-sufficient in as much as possible, eliminating excessive price-motivated trade, which is only a race to the bottom. We have a history of imperialism, where tyranny and repression are employed in all their possible forms to maintain a source of cheap products and cheap labour. This needs to stop. We need fair trade.

Today's global monetary and trade wars are not globalism or global development, at least before Trump. Rather, they are new forms of global economic imperialism that seek to make every economic unit in the world inoperable and rendered totally dependent on trade, thus also dependent on the elite. The objective that emerges is that people would become net consumers. This modern imperialism is hostile towards people, small businesses, human rights, and the environment, although they will tell you the opposite. Climate religion, with its proposed taxes, is just one more strategy to consolidate the power of the elite by restructuring the economy in favour of control by ideological elite, and the outcome will be poverty for the people. This needs to stop, and it can be stopped without being socialist. I think the socialism developing today is social welfare for global capitalism and its elite. There is not much difference between communism and capitalism; they are becoming the same tyranny. All ideology brings the same end.

An asset-driven economy is not socialism; it is covenantal, a pure form of capitalism that through its covenant includes all people in the production of wealth by recognizing foundational assets such as objective justice, real human rights, and objective reality as having as much or more value to the economy than any or all intellectual property. It is by the use of this value that we can make a monetary system that is sustainable and reciprocal.

The next time the Feds need to rescue the monetary system with trillions of dollars of quantitative easing, do not entice us to borrow more money. Just send us a cheque; we will look after it. And yes, keep the cheques coming until we have re-established a good balance between savings and debt. After that it should be smooth running for everyone and no longer ad hoc monetarism.

All those foreign states, allies, and friends in the world with developing economies and dependent on the International Monetary Fund should also be included providing they have a good business plan, one that begins with objective reality, objective human rights, Justice and a government committed to maintaining the Covenant value for money.

I was checking some of my facts on internet and discovered that more people are thinking of a similar quantitative easing approach, recognizing the same problem with quantitative easing for which I have been building a historic case. They refer to it as "positive money" and "helicopter money," a system of the Central Banks making direct payments to households to stimulate the economy. Two of the economists making the argument for this are Mark Blyth and Eric Lonergan.

I am arguing for a constitutional monetary system that is permanent and will always include the people, and where money is on an established foundation for value that will make it universal and interchangeable with other states. I take the Covenant approach because I know all good things can also be used for the worst evil. Therefore, in a Covenant relationship, there is equality and a reciprocal balance between obligation and benefit that is effectual and recognizable, that can be protected from abuse. We do not need a secretive ad hoc monetary system.

What needs to happen today? Today we have a crony monetarism that is monetary welfare for capitalism and more debt for the poor. We have crony governments pandering to big business and elitist ideology and alternate realities. We have aspiring crony socialism, where everything is free, which actually means no obligation no responsibility and no contribution. We have crony justice pandering to ideology and alternate realities but not defending the Constitution. Instead, they make an ideological imposition on the Constitution.

The austerity of the European Union suddenly fell off the face of the earth because it came to realize it was political poison and would kill it. In like manner, all the cronyism I have just mentioned also needs to fall off the face of the earth. How do you think any of this derangement is not also political suicide? We, the Western nations, need leadership grounded in objective reality.

The quantitative easing in the United States after the monetary crisis of 2008 is said to be about 4.5 trillion dollars over the following 5 years. How beneficial was it? It stimulated the economy by inflating assets with the monetary value of attrition; billionaires became greater billionaires by attrition value. My own property increased in value by 300 per cent, all attributable to the attrition of money. Now what do those get who do not own property or a home, who rent? How do they share in the attrition of our money? Rent increases to cover the return on the added value for the property, payable to the landlord? In all fairness, the Federal Reserve should be sending all of these tenants a cheque. Or do we now only allow property owners to participate in the State?

When the poor are included in the creation of capital and wealth, it should be a very significant move towards the elimination of crime, at least poor people's crimes. Shall we yet object that money would corrupt the poor? Better pile it up on the billionaires as there it would be more effective. There is a whole generation of young people emerging who may never be able to afford any property at all. They will choose communism, Marxism or socialism, not because it is better, but out of spite for not being included in the State. Our crony ideological capitalism can only blame itself. We need to change the monetary system - it needs to reflect reality.

I love the Covenant, the supremacy of God, and the rule of law: "I will be your God, you will be my People." When we are objective concerning God's creation, we won't be looking for alternate reality but discovering the reality that exists. We would be learning from the past to have better expectations for the future. We would not be trying to sanitize or rewrite our history to suit our alternate reality; we would be learning from it for what it is, the good, the bad, the ugly. Without true knowledge, we perish. Imitation knowledge is derangement.

What are my expectations for what I have just written? I started out looking for the origins and cause for anti-Semitism, and I end up writing a defence for the Covenant including a covenantal monetary system. When we, the nation of the Covenant, can work together and even become a majority, we can achieve a lot. Then I am also sure that our enemies and those who hate us will all but dismiss this as one more Zionist conspiracy to take over the world.

There is no synthesis between the biblical Covenant of Grace and the Social Contract of ideological paganism. There is no social or economic synthesis in contradictions. There are no syntheses between reality and alternate reality. We should have known this already from the history of the Maccabean wars, where the Greeks tried to convert the Jews to paganism. Now, 2,200 years later, we are again trying to achieve the same tyranny. You would think we would learn from history.

While the twentieth century was bad in terms of human suffering caused by Ideology and its alternate realities, the twenty-first century is shaping up to look like it could be much worse. How big do you want this tragedy to be? The longer we delay in opposing ideology the greater it will be. We need a major repentance and return to the Covenant. We owe it to the family, the nation, and God.

Sorry for having reached so deep into the basket of deplorables. But we have a long memory. Today is payback time, while there is yet the opportunity, and again, we can give you the very best. It is worth more than gold. The Covenant.

Here, at the end of this book, I have one request because when we do not ask, we do not get. There is this quote from the Bible that is as much secular and civil as it is religious and spiritual that I will also use here: "We have not because we ask not; we ask amiss, we ask to consume upon our lusts" (James 4:4 AKJV). Having this in mind, I will ask. Our request is for a better monetary system that will include everyone, including tenants and the poor in the creation of monetary wealth that is not all debt but also drawn from the capital of objective civil life as asset money. The deal is this: We will put an end to all violent crime, an end to the drug trade, and an end to drug dependency. We will be mothers and fathers to our children and build up the family, the community, and the nation. We will put away idolatry, ideology, and all alternate realities. Why would anyone engage in crime when we can be gainfully employed in stewardship and engaged in the creation of monetary, economic, social and spiritual wealth?

We will take the Covenant, live the Covenant, and seek the Lord our God for His mercy endures forever; redeeming the cause of misery – our sin - in the Redeemer – our God.

The End
Cornelius Van Blyderveen

APPENDIX 1

Protest

I think I need to be clear about my intentions at the beginning – in publishing this book – before I get accused of enticing all kinds of horrible things.

People have a propensity to protest when things do not go right – some people more than others – and today's time of unrest appears on edge for protest. We need to be proactive and take control of the situation with a real solution. The past unrest, of occupy Wall Street and defund the police are big on finding fault - fault that may be genuine but often misguided – and no real solution is put forward.

My book is offered as the solution, that is why I wrote it – the Covenant applied in life has been and always will be the solution. We can learn from our history that the benefit received from it is in accordance to the degree it is applied. We need a revival.

Self-defence begins with freedom of speech – putting forth a covenantal solution – with peaceful protest and demonstration (such also happens to be a self evident and logical requirement of the Covenant). To be peaceful takes strength. Let them first try to kill us for being peaceful. We are not an ideological mob. Burning down our neighbourhoods, looting and violence is anarchy and not protest. This works into the hands of the ideological elite, and is what they want and are looking for, and will entice.

Protest should not be exclusive; we included and support

everyone and every movement that defends the constitution and real human rights.

We need to protest the systemic ideological elitism in our universitie academia; it is the place where systemic is a problem.

In our day the greatest threat to peaceful protest and demonstration are the counter demonstrations and the infiltration from anarchists, (extremes from any opinion and fantasy), who will try to provoke violence and property damage, turning any protest into a propaganda victory for the ideological elite who are desperate to demonize us. We need to be vigilant about this. We need to be clear with law enforcement on what our intentions are. With Ideological government there is also the danger that we will get ideologically vetted law enforcement; before that happens we need to evangelize law enforcement with the Covenant. Covenant values establish their lawful existence and are in their own best interest.

Protest and demonstrations in the street may be a part of the strategy but they will Not win the war. We need to win back our communities, expand the base for the Covenant. We need to defund ideology in money and votes. We should not patronize ideology but flee from it and leave the ideologist isolated. I hope my book may work for you to that end. Take it where you thought you could never go. The world is opening up for change.

If you are going to protest and demonstrate and feel passionate about these issues, this is my permission - and some guidelines you need to follow. The first message we will convey - this is a peaceful protest, demonstration, of Civil liberty and freedom of speech. We will never allow the shutdown of freedom of speech. Never harass or provoke law enforcement, when you disagree with law enforcement retreat, and don't enter anything that may appear as entrapment. Use civil speech at all times, I abhor profane speech and I don't want it representing our cause.

The following slogans you may use coming from my book and others; Covenantal Money – Constitutional Money - Monetary Democracy – The Covenant – Take the Covenant – We follow the science not Ideology – All lives Mater – No Court Packing with Ideology – Justice not Ideology – Defend the Constitution – Real Human Rights not ideology – Freedom of Speech – Cornelius – The Cornelius Reformation.

The Iconic image on the cover of this book represents me but I think it stands more for peaceful protest – that is what I intend- let it stand as a symbol of this argument for the Covenant. I have a copyright on the image but you may use it together with the slogans I have listed above to make signs for your own use. For any commercial use you will need to ask permission. To use this image with slogan other than the ones approved above is forbidden unless permission is given. You have fair use to criticise the image but not misrepresent it.

Yes, you may simply use my logo for this book, the name Cornelius with the image, not that I want to get anything out of it for myself, but it is fitting from a Biblical perspective, from Cornelius mentioned in the New Testament of the Bible in Acts 10, which is a confirmation of the Covenant of Grace for the entire world. Yes, in that sense we need a Cornelius Reformation, and as for me its fine, that I would be eclipsed by the Scriptures.

APPENDIX 2

Ayn Rand - Objectivism

For all of you who are familiar with the philosophy of Ayn Rand's objectivism, you might ask what influence her philosophy has on my ideas of objectivism. I was not aware of Ayn Rand during the time I developed my ideas and wrote my book. I discovered her now, once my book was completed and in the process of being published; at times it may be good not to be overly educated, you might be a better juror.

To date all I know of her is what I have seen on podcasts from Jordan Peterson and the Ayn Rand Institute.

My objectivism is entirely developed through my search for the origin and cause of anti-Semitism from history. In this sense my ideas are original. My objectivism is grounded, first, on the reality of God and God's creation - as reality exists – and as God has said it was good; Second, the self-evident discovery and revelation, of the covenantal relationship with God, reality and man for value and self-preservation. The common good can only be discovered in this covenantal relationship with reality.

In this covenantal relationship, objective self preservation and value will always prevail as the consensus of the common good, it will always overcome subjectivism – truth makes us free because it destroys our lies. The only time subjectivism can prevail is when the tyranny of subjectivism restrains and forbids objective truth, which requires denying the covenant. In civil relationships truth and value are objective because nothing else is sustainable in a long term conscientious thought process. This truth is very distressing for subjectivism and collectivism. (This is the reason why constitutional government, human rights and democracy have been so rare throughout our history).

Than it also follows, anti-Semitism is also anti-objectivism and anti-covenant. There is a relationship between anti-Semitism and objectivism. A society that is more objective in outlook will be more covenantal and less anti-Semitic. A society that is subjective in outlook will be tyrannical and both anti-covenant, and anti-Semitic.

It is unfortunate for Ayn Rand that she, like Karal Marx appears to have a personal vendetta with their Jewish religion, that she denies faith and rejects God, and then also as well the covenant. By doing so the ideal person for her is left standing as a rational, objective individual of capitalist greed and selfishness; something her critics like to point out. Her critics need to consider what successful greed and selfishness is or looks like. They are subjective terms. Successful greed and selfishness is subjective privilege for the self. This to me looks an awful lot like the critics and their philosophy themselves with their collectivism. Collectivism does not preclude greed, selfishness or privilege.

Had, Ayn Rand recognized the truth of her own religion and its faith she could have offered the covenant as the objective solution to collectivism. In the words of Ayn Rand "there is no such thing as a collective brain", (as selfish collectivism would have); but there is a consensus of objective truth in a covenantal relationship concerning value and self-preservation, that can be realized. She defends many of the benefits from the covenant and then in the end appears to side with tyranny.

Wikipedia tries to sum up the essence of Ayn Rand's philosophy with a quote from her "if one recognizes the supremacy of reason and applies it consistently all the rest follows". How does one recognize reason without first believing the context for it, such as reality – its objectivity –and our relationship with it? Despite what she may say about faith, I think she believes a lot. We need the faith to believe that we can believe, and how is empirical evidence meaningful when there is nothing to believe?

Ayn Rand is a classic example of the Jewish tragedy, rejecting the covenant, not comprehending the covenant, or not recognizing a covenant obscured by ideological religion. This also is the greatest Christian tragedy.

God does not expect us to comprehend Him, the supernatural, or even the miracles in the Bible, but we are expected to comprehend the concepts of the Covenant of Grace, they are objective and real, intended for our good and salvation; A priori for knowledge. We all utilize the Covenant of Grace in faith for its benefits until it helps us discover our cherished lies, then we become offended.

The Covenant requires reason and logic for repentance and restoration to achieve peace - and peace is objective. If you think there is a subjective peace, it confirms the objective peace (repentance is peace). Peace is complete; it is not divided or characterized.

"......Come now, and let us reason together, saith the Lord: though your sins be as scarlet, they shall be white as snow; though they be red like crimson they shall be as wool"....... Isaiah 1: 18 AKJV

APPENDIX 3

President Mitterrand's Speech

As I said earlier I found this speech from president Francois Mitterrand, on VIE Publique au Coeur du debat public, since president Mitterrand died in 1995, I have asked them for permission to republish the speech in my book, the answer I got was - there may be copyrights on the material they publish and I should ask the author and in this case the President of France. I sent an email to President Emmanuel Macron. The reply I got back, directed me to apply to the French National Archives, which I did and that appears to be a difficult automated process characterized by "we are all busy call back later".

Wither I get permission or not in the future, I will rely on fair use for giving you this beautiful speech. I find it to be current News because it is very relevant to the social political environment of today, (we have a tendency to repeat the tragedies in history). I ground my permission on Mitterrand's own words as he ended the speech, "There is only one duty left: that of teaching it to those who will follow us". I will take him up on that duty.

President Emmanuel Macron has publicly said that American academia's – woke - from critical race theory is not welcome in France. I think he would recognize that Mitterrand's speech is relevant to this issue.

As descendants from French Huguenots and a recipient of the

apology, I would think we would have the benefit from this apology in its use and not have it revoked from us as if it would no longer be valid.

Notwithstanding this I did check out French copyright laws, and I found Article L122 – 5, define the exceptions to French copyright law, which are relatively restricted, but do establish a fair use.

"Once a work has been published the author cannot prevent, in cases where the name of the author and source are clearly indicated.

A, Analyses and short citations justified by the critical, polemical, scientific or pedagogical nature of the work

B, Press reviews

C, Diffusion of public speeches as currant news".

BIBLIOGRAPHY - FOR FURTHER READING

Classic Books

The Bible, Authorized King James version 1610, publisher Trinitarian Bible Society, London UK

The Jerusalem Bible, First book of the Maccabees and the second Book of the Maccabees second century BC, Readers Edition 1966, Doublday and Company Inc. New York

The Heidelberg Catechism, Zacharian Ursinus, Casper Olevianus, Heidelberg University, 1568

Westminster Confession of Faith, 1647, Approved by the General Assembly 1647, and ratified and established by acts of Parliament 1649 and 1690 as the public and avowed confession of the Church of Scotland, with the proofs from the Scripture. Reprinted, Free Presbyterian Publications, Bell and Brain Ltd. Glasgow Scotland 2003

Lex Rex (The Law is King), Samuel Rutherford, Limited government and constitutionalism, 1644 monergism.com

The works of Josephus, Flavius Josephus (AD37 – c100) complete and unabridged, translated by William Whiston . Hendrickson publishing, USA, 1987

Boot, Joseph, Why I still believe. The Ezra Institute, Baker Books, Grand Rapids Michigan, 2005

Boot, Joseph, How Than Shall we Answer? The Ezra Institute, New Wine Press West Sussex UK, 2008

Boot, Joseph, the Mission of God, a Manifestation of Hope, The Ezra Institute, Freedom Press St. Catharines, On. Canada 2014

Baruch Maoz, Judaism is not Jewish, a Friendly Critique of the Messianic Movement, Christian focus Publications, Bell and Bain Glasgow, Scotland, 2003

Blomqvsit,Wonnacott, Wonnacott, Economics, second Canadian edition, McGraw-Hill Ryerson Limited 1987,

Berger, Josef, Discoveries of the New World, American Heritage Publishing Co. Inc. New York, 1960

Black, Conrad, The Canadian Manifesto, how one frozen country can save the world, Sutherland House Inc. Canada 2018 by permission page 94,95,97 (2021-01-20)

Bodoff, Lippman, The Binding Of Isaac, Religious murders, and Kabbalah, seeds of Jewish extremism and alienation. Devora Publishing Jerusalem, Israel, 2005

Dimont Max. I, Jews, God and History, 2nd edition, New American Library New York, 1962

Fishwick, D., Wilkinson B., Cairns J.C., The Foundations of the West. St. Michael's College, University of Toronto, Clarke, Irwin & Company, 1963

Galbraith, John Kenneth, The culture of Contentment. Houghton Mifflin Company, New York, 1992

Hardy, W. G., Our Heritage from the Past. The Canadian Publishers, Toronto, 1964

Harvey, David, Spaces of Global Capitalism, toward a theory of uneven geographical development. Verso, London UK 2006

(The) Jewish Philosophy Reader. Edited by Daniel H. Frank,

Oliver Leaman and Charles H. Manekin, Routledge, London UK, 2000

Kant, Immanuel, (1724 – 1804) Basic writings of Kant. Edited and introduction by Allen W. Wood, Modern Library, New York, 2001

Kuiper, B. K. The Church in History. William B. Eerdmans Publishing Company, Grand Rapids, 1951

Locke, John (1632 – 1704) an Essay Concerning Human Understanding and an Essay Concerning the True Original, Extent and End of Civil Government. The English Philosophers from Beacon to Mill, Edited with an introduction by Edward A. Burtt, Cornell University, Random House, 1939

Lonergan, Eric, Money. Routledge, New York USA, 2009

Phillips, Kevin, Bad Money, reckless finance, failed political and the global crisis of American capitalism. Viking, Penguin Group, New York, 2008

Saul, John, Ralston, The Collapse of Globalism and the reinvention of the world. Viking Canada, Penguin Group, 2005

Schaeffer, Francis A. How shall we than Live? The rise and fall of Western Thought and Culture. Crossway, Illinois USA 1976

Smith, Adam, The Nature and Cause of Wealth of Nations. 1776, introduction by Tom Butler – Bowdon 2010

Solzhenitsyn, Aleksandr, I. The Gulag Archipelago. Harper and Row Publishers, New York, 1973

Steger, Manfred, B. Globalization, A very short introduction. Oxford University Press, 2003

Trump, Donald J., Crippled America, how to make America great again. Threshold Editions, New York, 2015

Trueman, John, The Enduring Past, revised edition. 1964, The Ryerson Press, Toronto, 1964

Montefiore, Simon Sebag, Jerusalem, the Biography. Vintage Books, Random House Inc. New York 2011

Internet

Aljazeera.com News, US Congressional Executive Commission on China, 2021-01-15

Azquotes.com, Henry Morgentelar

Balmer, Randy, Under Trump the American Religious Right is rewriting its code of Ethics. Dartmouth College. The Guardian, 2019-02-18

Canada Hansard, No. 110, June 11 2008 (39.2)

CBC NL Newfoundland and Labrador, Full apology ceremony for resident school survivors; Last viewed 2021-01-19

Durham, Graham, Olympic advice on Transgender athletes due after Tokyo Games. Associate press, March 4 2020 Washington times.com, 2021-01-30

Macleans.ca, Apology, Residents Schools Servivors. Catherine McIntyre 2017-11-04

Meister, Stanley, 300 year old decree seen now as shameful, France recalls ban of Protestants. Los Angeles Times, 1985-10-18

Protestant Church and the Nazi state, Holocaust and Human behavior. Facinghistory.org, December 2020

Starkey, David, Where Woke Culture Comes From. trigernometry, youtub, December 2020

Time line of Influenza, Wikipedia.ca American virologist Ron Fouchier and Yoshihiro Kawaoka intentionally develop a strain bassed on H5N1 for which no vaccine exists, causing outrage both in the media and scientific community Wikipedia.ca

Influenza deaths in Canada 2019, statistical reports that the death rate for influenza and pneumonia in Canada rages from 16.1 to 23 deaths per 100,000 over the period of 2000 to 2018. Statista.com

Science magazine, Controversial experiments that could make bird flu more risky poised to resume. Jocelyn Kaiser, 2019-01-08

Ethical Alternatives to Experiments with Novel Potential Pandemic Pathogens. Marc Lipsitch – Aison Galvani, Journals.plos. org May 20 2014

Wilson, William D., The Orthodox Betrayal; How German Christians Embraced and Taught Nazism and sparked a Christian Battle. Georgia South University, 2016 December 2020

Critical race theory, Wikipedia.com, Britannica.com, Encycopedia .com

Archeological sites

Western Wall, Jerusalem, Israel
Chichen Itza, Mexico

Printed in the United States
by Baker & Taylor Publisher Services